Putting Tanzania's Hidden Economy to Work

Reform, Management, and Protection of its Natural Resource Sector

THE WORLD BANK
Washington, D.C.

ISBN-13: 978-0-8213-7462-7
eISBN: 978-0-8213-7463-4
ISSN: 0253-2123   DOI: 10.1596/978-0-8213-7462-7

Library of Congress Cataloging-in-Publication Data has been requested.

Contents

LIST OF TABLES

LIST OF FIGURES

Foreword

This study assesses the paths among natural resources, growth, and poverty. It reveals a "hidden economy" in Tanzania's natural resources, one that is unseen in traditional analyses, but one, when brought into the light, shows great potential for nurturing growth and ending poverty.

The report is direct. It emphasizes stopping corruption by fighting crime and bettering governance. It calls for an end to price distortions—for better capture of resource rents and for less waste of resources. It explores the idea of safety nets in resource sectors. These might include: co-management for sustainable resource use; training for durable social networks; and diversification of livelihoods to reduce dependency on a single sector.

The World Bank has been active in policy and institutional reforms in resource sectors. We commend the Government of Tanzania for its efforts to build better institutions and to improve accountability. These include stronger institutions in forestry and an Amended Deep Sea Fishing Authority (DSFA) which formalizes revenue sharing between the mainland and Zanzibar. We hope that the findings presented in this volume will help to cut waste and inefficiency and thereby allow Tanzania's natural resources to contribute more to growth and poverty reduction.

John Murray McIntire
Country Director for Tanzania and Uganda
The World Bank

Acknowledgments

The research leading to this report was initiated as a part of the CEM process for Tanzania to understand more fully, the linkages between environment, natural resources and growth. The work was started as a joint initiative by AFTS2 and AFTP2 under the Co-Task Team Leadership of Indu Hewawasam (Senior Environmental Specialist) and Robert Utz (Senior Country Economist). We launched the research in collaboration with the Development Partner Group on Environment and Natural Resources (DPG-ENR) in Tanzania. COWI International (Tanzania) was contracted to carry out the study, to which many members of the Development Partner Group on Environment and Natural Resources (DPG-ENR) and counterparts in government contributed. The summary of the findings were incorporated as a chapter within the Country Economic Memorandum.

Given the importance of sound governance of natural resources to growth and the poverty reduction agenda, we supported further research into the initial findings. This second phase of the research was carried out by Jack Ruitenbeek and Cynthia Cartier, who are the main authors of this current report. The current version has benefitted from the findings of the background study by COWI International (Tanzania), comments and contributions from a number of sources, and independent field research. Comments and contributions were received from: the United Republic of Tanzania led by the Ministry of Natural Resources and Tourism, Co-Task Team Leaders, Sector Management and the Tanzania Country Management Unit, Kirk Hamilton (Lead Environmental Specialist), Christopher Sheldon, Leopoldo Maraboli, Christian Peter, Jane Kibbassa and members of the DPG-ENR. This Analytical work was carried out under the general supervision of Karen Brooks, Kathleen Krumm, and Marjory-Anne Bromhead (Sector Managers).

We are grateful for all comments and contributions. The recommendations and observations in this paper remain those of the Task Managers and authors, and do not necessarily reflect the opinions of the World Bank Group or other individuals.

Abbreviations

ACM	Adaptive Co-Management
ASM	Artisanal and Small-scale Mining
ASMs	Artisanal and Small-scale Miners
CDM	Clean Development Mechanism
CPUE	Catch Per Unit Effort
DDI	Diamond Development Initiative
DFOB	Director of Forestry and Beekeeping
DSFA	Deep Sea Fishing Authority
EEZ	Exclusive Economic Zone
ER	Emission Reduction
EU	European Union
FBD	Forestry and Beekeeping Division
FEMATA	Federation of Miners Associations of Tanzania
GDP	Gross Domestic Product
GEF	Global Environment Facility
GIS	Geographical Information System
GNI	Gross National Income
GPS	Global Positioning System (satellite)
IOTC	Indian Ocean Tuna Commission
MACEMP	Marine and Coastal Environment Management Project
MALE	Ministry of Agriculture, Lands and Environment [Zanzibar]
MCS	Monitoring, Control and Surveillance
MDG	Millennium Development Goal
MEM	Ministry of Energy and Minerals
MLF	Marine Legacy Fund
MNRT	Ministry of Natural Resources and Tourism
MRD	Mineral Resources Department
MSY	Maximum Sustainable Yield
NFP	National Forest Programme
NGO	Non-Governmental Organization
NSSF	National Social Security Fund
NTFP	Non-Timber Forest Product
PFA	Private Fisheries Agreement
PORALG	President's Office Regional Administration and Local Government
REMA	Regional Miners Associations
RFO	Regional Fisheries Organization
SADC	Southern African Development Community
TAFIRI	Tanzania Fisheries Research Institute
TAMIDA	Tanzania Mineral Dealers Association
TANAPA	Tanzania National Parks
TASAF	Tanzania Social Action Fund
TAWICO	Tanzania Wildlife Corporation
TAWIRI	Tanzania Wildlife Research Institute

TAWOMA	Tanzania Women's Mining Association
TIST	The International Small Group & Tree Planting Program
TSh	Tanzania Shilling
TWRAS	Tanzania Water Resources Assistance Strategy
UCLAS	University College of Lands and Architectural Studies
UNCLOS	United Nations Convention on the Law of the Sea
URT	United Republic of Tanzania
WD	Wildlife Division [of MNRT]
WMA	Wildlife Management Area
WSS	Water Supply and Sanitation

Introduction

In recent years, Tanzania's annual real economic growth rate has been between 6 and 7 percent with GNI equivalent to about US$340 per person. In addition, a "hidden" economy could potentially have contributed an additional US$100 per person. This hidden economy is hidden only to the extent that it does not obviously contribute to the official statistics or to the national treasury. In fact, this economy is a core element of Tanzania's well-being. It employs and provides subsistence for millions, it nurtures the environment on which all of Tanzania's citizenry's health depends, and it provides the basis for much of the economic growth in the formal—unhidden—economy. It is hidden from our books, but not hidden from our view. "It" is, in short, the natural resource sector.

However, natural resources are an obvious positive contributor to economic output, generating exports from traditional activities such as forestry, fisheries, mining, and wildlife. Moreover, 582,000 tourists visited the United Republic of Tanzania (URT) in 2004, contributing some US$746 million to export earnings. This is just the tip of the iceberg. Hidden values and untapped potential remain uncounted. A recent single shipment of illegal ivory left Tanga port valued at US$200 million. Fishing in the Exclusive Economic Zone in 2004 contributed in excess of US$300 million to foreign coffers, but less than 2 percent found its way back to Tanzanian hands. Upwards of half a million artisanal miners make a living in the shadows of their larger corporate counterparts, with most of the small-scale production leaving the country un-noticed, and untaxed. It is this hidden part of the economy—the uncounted, the illegal, the unnoticed, or the squandered—that is the topic of this paper.

While some parts of this natural resource trade are hidden only from the formal economy—because of improper pricing or lack of well-functioning markets—many parts are also hidden from the rule of law. Corruption, cronyism, and coverup have become a systemic malaise in some parts of this hidden economy. Management under such circumstances is short-sighted and favors the powerful, further contributing to real imbalances in income and contributing to, rather than alleviating, conditions of poverty that still pervade in the country. Coupled with the various pricing distortions and policy failures, such corruption in itself becomes self-reinforcing, with police and politicians as likely to be implicated in scandal as are common business people or foreign entrepreneurs. The hidden economy becomes a self-contained, self-serving system. If such a system served the benefit of all Tanzanians, then it might be tolerated. It does, after all, provide low-cost charcoal, cheap fishery and bushmeat protein, and subsistence livelihoods for millions. However, the path is not sustainable. The fish will disappear, the water will dry up, the soil will become infertile, and the social fabric itself will start to unravel if circumstances continue unchecked. Corruption, policy failure, and price distortions all contribute—in a complex but deterministic web—to undermining the natural resource sector on which Tanzania, ultimately, depends.

This paper tells a story about conditions in this hidden economy—the parts of the natural resource sector often ignored in conventional economic analyses and studies—and makes recommendations for future policy actions. The paper draws primarily from extensive background studies undertaken of the Forestry, Fishery, Wildlife, Mining, and Tourism subsectors (COWI 2005) as well as a wide range of complementary studies undertaken by the World Bank and others.[1] It de-emphasizes those sectors with factors of production that are not readily traded or exported (such as land and water), although some examples are given relating to soil quality and water management based on extensive studies undertaken within the agriculture and water sectors. The story is relatively simple: pricing distortions, coupled with institutional weakness and the lack of rule of law, have created an environment that undermines economic growth. Examples from the various sectors will tell this same story—albeit in different ways.

This paper also acknowledges that Tanzania has already taken positive steps to making some of the needed corrections to protect its natural resources. In recent analyses of corruption indicators world-wide (World Bank Institute 2006), Tanzanian stands out among those nations as having made significant progress towards improving accountability and reducing economic leakages. Anti-corruption legislation was drafted for parliament attention in early 2007. Revisions to the Deep Sea Fishing Authority Act were passed into law in early 2007. Moreover, changes in institutional arrangements, taxation, and general management of the resource sector show promise and have contributed positively to general economic growth. Yet, the sector remains fragile and vulnerable in other respects: perceptions of unequal income distribution, impacts of climate change, and other external influences must also be addressed to build on past successes. Complacency is not an option at this stage.

---

1. Sources are provided at the end of the paper. In addition to the COWI background reports, this paper draws extensively on internal working papers of the World Bank including: notes from a mining project appraisal; forestry project Mid-Term Review and supervision reports; MACEMP supervision reports; and the Tanzania water strategy background papers. Material relating to corruption and governance is based on studies undertaken through the World Bank Institute.

The recommendations are relatively straightforward. The paper recommends a three-pillared approach that we characterize as follows:

I. Reforming Tanzania's Hidden Economy—Eliminating Corruption.
II. Managing Tanzania's Hidden Economy—Allowing the Natural Resource Sector to Contribute to Economic Growth and Poverty Alleviation.
III. Protecting Tanzania's Economy—Promoting Resilience and Reducing Vulnerability in the Natural Resource Sector.

The first pillar—reform—focuses squarely on eliminating corruption and improving transparency. Its elements will be driven principally by political will, but concentrate on eliminating illegal activities, improving accountability, and enhancing the information base for monitoring and compliance. Specific potential interventions relate to training, institutional capacity building and reform, and improved transparency within decisionmaking and monitoring mechanisms.

The second pillar—management—focuses on more traditional sectoral resource management, such as elimination of price distortions, capture of resource rents, and reduction of waste and externalities. Some of these management interventions also imply institutional changes to permit a more efficient, and more equitable, distribution of benefits. Specific interventions relate to clarification and entrenchment of property rights, improved resource pricing, removal of distorting taxes and subsidies, and supportive institutional restructuring.

The third pillar—protection—is less familiar to many planners, but critical within the context of economic planning in a complex yet vulnerable natural resource sector. The reality is that the sector has become less resilient to external shocks, and such shocks (such as fishery collapses, droughts, tsunamis, extinction, avian flu) are becoming part of the experience and living memory of the current generation of Tanzanians. Such shocks also exacerbate social inequalities, which in turn can lead to increased conflict over scarce resources; the conflict invariably leads to resource management inefficiencies and concomitant economic losses. In the same way that Tanzania is putting into place social safety nets for its labor force (NSSF), there are also appropriate safety net mechanisms and strategies available for protecting the natural resource sector. Many interventions associated with protection may be equally considered as means for improving institutional effectiveness or general resource management. Within the context of this paper, however, we will draw particular attention to: revenue retention schemes as a mechanism for reducing social vulnerability; co-management arrangements for improving response times; education and awareness for strengthening social networks; the implementation of vulnerability monitoring systems; and various diversification measures for reducing vulnerability to single-sector shocks.

The organization of this paper is as follows. Chapter 1 provides background information relating to conditions within the hidden economy, characterizing its contribution to economic output and social well-being. Chapter 2 focuses on the reform agenda to address current lapses in governance. Chapter 3 provides prescriptions relating to sustainable resource management, looking at traditional sectors mentioned above as well as some of the emerging resource-based sectors (notably, carbon finance linked to the Clean

Development Mechanism of the Kyoto Protocol). Chapter 4 explores in greater detail the need and opportunities for safety net interventions to improve the resilience of the sector; it also highlights how water sector management is being used as a central theme in establishing some safety nets. Chapter 5 recaps by providing a summary of key recommendations, and an action plan associated with these recommendations. An Appendix provides a "sector-at-a-glance" summary of recommended or potential intervention candidates by category.

CHAPTER 1

The Big Picture: Tanzania's Hidden Economy

Tanzanians can be proud of their country's achievements over the past ten years. Economic growth has been the envy of the region. Foreign investment has increased as domestic investment conditions have become more favorable. Poverty incidence has been reduced. Corruption has declined. Yet, significant challenges remain, especially in the natural resource sector. Population growth and migration continues to place limited land and water resources under non-sustainable pressures. Uncertain or absent property rights contribute to situations of open access or resource use conflict. External influences—ranging from climate variation to foreign-owned fishing fleets—threaten the long-term existence of some resources. Revenue sharing from existing resource stocks is frequently perceived as inequitable. In this chapter, we will take stock of the economic contribution of some of the key natural resource sectors, looking at both the obvious economic contributions of the sector as well as some of the unaccounted contributions. In so doing, we will take a first glance at various resource development issues that contribute to sectoral weaknesses, and identify potential general means for addressing these weaknesses. Subsequent chapters will take up each of these themes and issues in greater detail. This chapter also provides some methodological context in terms of valuation of unaccounted values, identifying the root causes for loss of value, and prescribing classes of interventions to address these root causes or weaknesses.

The Natural Resource Sector: A First Look at the Obvious

Tanzania as a whole remains a relatively impoverished country. Its 38 million inhabitants live in a low-income class country; in 2005 the Gross National Income (GNI) per capita was only US$340. Some 36 percent of the population remained at the national poverty line, and many of the social indicators reflect this poverty. The literacy rate is only 70 percent, life expectancy at birth is under 50 years, and HIV prevalence is at about 7 percent of the adult population (age 15–49). The economy has been growing and conditions are, in some cases, getting better. Population growth has fallen to below 2 percent annually, while GDP growth over the past five years has averaged about 7 percent annually. Primary school enrollments have been rising, and now stand at close to 100 percent. The country is very dynamic, as investment has noticeably increased. It will be challenging for Tanzania to meet many of the various Millennium Development Goals (MDGs), yet there is room for cautious optimism in some areas. Preliminary results from the 2004 Demographic and Health Survey suggest that considerable progress was made in the reduction of malnutrition and child mortality. Simulations show that the income poverty and hunger MDGs may be attainable if Tanzania is able to continue with its episode of medium high growth and with its improvements in the social sectors (Table 1.1).

Within this context, natural resources in Tanzania constitute a significant, albeit fragile, wealth asset. Since 1996, mining, fisheries, and tourism have been the most dynamic sectors in the economy. While tourism development is a success story in macroeconomic terms, significant potential still exists to generate local development spin-offs. Most known mineral deposits are already being tapped, but new mineral stocks are being discovered. The fisheries sector is still growing, but there are signs of decline in the catch per unit effort in Lake Victoria and in the catch of fish and prawn in the coastal zones; this points toward a deceleration of growth in the medium and long terms. Forestry, wildlife, and offshore fisheries resources, though declining, are still relatively abundant and have largely untapped growth potential.

The best way to capture this natural resource potential is not necessarily simple. The National Strategy for Growth and Poverty Reduction of 2005 subscribes to the principles of sustainable and equitable development. The operational starting points of these principles include the following:

- Renewable resources should be exploited on the bases of maximizing profits and sustaining yields. Resources should not be driven to extinction, regardless of the dictates of present value maximization. Hence, harvesting rates should not exceed regeneration rates and waste emissions should not exceed absorptive capacities.
- Nonrenewable resources should be exploited at a rate equal to the creation of renewable substitutes. Revenue from the exploitation of nonrenewable resources should contain an income component and a capital component. The capital component should be used to invest in building up a new renewable asset to replace the nonrenewable one at the point of its exhaustion.
- Revenue generated from natural resources should be shared equitably, in particular with the rural communities on whose land these resources are located.

These macroeconomics of sustainability require integrating qualitative development and growth in gross domestic product (GDP) more fully, giving equal weight to the need for pro-poor growth and the maintenance of a sustainable natural resource base. Because of policy failures, Tanzania's natural resource endowments are not harnessed in an optimal way to achieve all of the country's development objectives.

Table 1.1. Tanzania MDG Baseline, Most Recent Estimate and Target

	Baseline	Most Recent	Target	Year of Baseline	Year Most Recent
Goal 1: eradicate extreme poverty and hunger					
Reduce extreme poverty by half					
—national poverty line	38.6%	35.6%	19.3%	1991	2000
—dollar-a-day poverty line	61.1%	57.5%	30.6%	1991	2000
Reduce hunger by half	29%	22%	14.5%	1991	2004
Goal 2: Achieve universal primary education					
Net enrollment in primary school	51%	91%	100%	1990	2004
Goal 3: Promote gender equality and empower women					
Equal girls' enrollment in primary school	1.01	0.99	1	1990	2004
Equal girls' enrollment in secondary school	0.70	0.81	1	1990	2000
Goal 4: Reduce child mortality					
Reduce child mortality of under fives by two thirds	141	112	47	1991	2004
Goal 5: Improve maternal health					
Reduce maternal mortality by three quarters*	529	578	132	1996	2004
Goal 6: Combat HIV/AIDS, malaria and other diseases					
Halt and reverse spread of AIDS	n.a.	7.0%			2003
Halt and reverse spread of malaria	21%	36%		1999	2004
Goal 7: Ensure environmental sustainability					
Halve proportion without improved drinking water in urban areas	13%	10%	7%	1991	2000
Halve proportion without improved drinking water in rural areas	65%	54%	33%	1991	2000
Halve proportion without sanitation in urban areas	2%	4%	1%	1991	2000
Halve proportion without sanitation in rural areas	9%	8%	5%	1991	2000

Source: World Bank, Tanzania Country Economic Memorandum (draft July 2006).

* Maternal mortality is a so-called low frequency event. Low frequency events are difficult to measure accurately in surveys like the DHS which serve as source for these estimates, as few cases of maternal mortality are registered. Consequently maternal mortality rates are associated with large confidence intervals and the observed maternal mortality rates of 529 in 1996 and 578 in 2004 are statistically not different.

As a starting point, however, we can look at the obvious contributions of this sector. Table 1.2 shows the relative contributions of the sectors traditionally associated with renewable natural resources from a government budget perspective. Even at this level, it is clear that although these sectors contribute to the economy, the institutions responsible

Table 1.2. MNRT Annual Revenue and Budget FY2004 (billion TSh)

	Revenue	Expenditures
Forestry/beekeeping	5.82	7.63
Wildlife	9.55	7.59
Fisheries	9.70	4.65
Tourism	0.96	2.88
Other	—	3.51
Total	26.03	26.26

Source: MNRT 2004.

Notes: This includes revenue collected and retained at source. Budget expenditures are recurrent amounts only.

for their oversight may not be operating optimally from a fiscal perspective. Expenditures and forestry and tourism, for example, exceed the direct revenue being generated for government. While investment in such sectors may be warranted because of their broader economic spin-offs, it raises issues relating to the sustainability of the institutional set-up in such cases. In the following summaries, we look briefly at the key institutional players and at the overall economic contribution of key sectors.

Fisheries

Tanzania's fishery sector is characterized by three regional fisheries: (i) a freshwater lake fishery with most production coming from Lake Victoria; (ii) a coastal fishery that encompasses artisanal demersal and pelagic fisheries accompanied by a commercial coastal prawn fishery; and, (iii) an offshore pelagic marine fishery dominated by foreign fishing vessels within the Exclusive Economic Zone (EEZ). Management of the sector on the mainland is undertaken by the Fisheries Division of MNRT, while on Zanzibar responsibility lies within the Ministry of Agriculture, Lands and Environment (MALE). Scientific assessments and input are conducted through the Tanzania Fisheries Research Institute (TAFIRI). Offshore marine fisheries fall under shared jurisdiction as a Union matter and will be governed under the Deep Sea Fishing Authority (DSFA) that will become operational in late 2006. The DSFA structure was catered for in the DSFA Act (1998) but revenue sharing arrangements that would permit operationalization have only been recently finalized; these were the subject of a Cabinet paper in 2006 and revisions to the DSFA Act were passed into law through a unanimous vote in Parliament in February 2007.

As a whole, the fisheries sector has grown at a rate of 6 to 7 percent annually since 2000. In 2004, revenue collection from fisheries amounted to TSh9.7 billion. About 80 percent of revenue comes from freshwater fisheries, with revenues from freshwater fisheries shared locally through revenue retention schemes. The 20 percent of revenues earned in marine fisheries are from licensing and various revenue sharing arrangements with foreign vessels. The number of foreign vessels licensed to operate in the EEZ on the mainland and

Zanzibar has increased from fewer than 10 in 1998 to more than 170 in 2004, corresponding to revenue of US$3.3 million. In terms of export earnings, fisheries contributed 10 percent of total exports in 2003 (US$130 million); the export value of Nile perch alone being US$100 million.

Forestry

Forestry resources on the mainland fall under the mandate of MNRT, with some control devolved to local government and the private sector. Institutional changes are underway with the transformation of the Forestry and Beekeeping Division into an Executive Agency. The reform of the Forestry sector over the last decade included the policy and legal framework, with a revision of the Forest Policy (1998) and the Forest Act (2002), which was enacted in 2004. Procedures and regulations for implementing the Act are currently under preparation. The Policy advocates private and community based Forestry and provides a legal basis for Joint Management of Forest reserves with catchment or biodiversity values. Much of the forest remains, in practice, under open access conditions.

There are a number of estimates of Tanzania's total forest cover and its rate of change. In 2001, the National Forest Programme estimated the country's forest and woodland resources at 33.5 million ha, which constitutes 38 percent of the total land area of Tanzania. The forest estate generally includes four areas. Most of the forest area is contained within Government forest reserves (15 million ha), of which 13 million ha are production forests distributed among 815 forest reserves. Some 600,000 ha of forest were owned and managed by local governments. Second, 83,000 ha are in government owned *industrial plantations*, distributed in 16 units throughout the country. Major plantation species are pines, cypress, eucalyptus and teak. Third, *private forestry* is practiced in community woodlots (70,000 to 150,000 ha) and private plantations. Finally, forests on *general lands* are classified under the Forest Policy, Land and Village Land Acts and were estimated in 2001 to cover 19 million ha. Because of the pressure on these forests for competing land uses (agriculture, livestock grazing, settlements and industrial development) the loss of forest cover is estimated to be high. For the country as a whole, the deforestation rate is estimated to be 91,276 ha per year (MNRT 2002).

In aggregate, forestry provided almost TSh6 billion in government revenue in 2004. It officially contributes 2 to 3 percent to GDP and 10 to 15 percent to export earnings.

Wildlife

The policy framework in Tanzania focuses mainly on wildlife conservation and not on utilization. The tradition of wildlife conservation in Tanzania dates back to the colonial era and the principle was manifested by former President Nyerere in the 1967 Arusha Declaration. Administration of wildlife resources in Tanzania falls within the Ministry of Natural Resources and Tourism. The two lead bodies under the Ministry are Tanzania National Parks (TANAPA) and the Wildlife Division (WD). Other institutions and parastatals include the Ngorongoro Conservation Authority, the Tanzania Wildlife Research Institute (TAWIRI), the Tanzania Wildlife Corporation (TAWICO) and the College of Wildlife Management at Mweka. In addition there is also administration through the district and regional administrative structures. The national legislation guiding the management of protected areas in Tanzania are the Wildlife Policy (1998) and the Wildlife Conservation Act (1974). The Wildlife Conservation Act is currently under revision.

The WD is responsible for wildlife conservation in Tanzania in game reserves, game controlled areas, open areas and district game reserves. The two main functions of the division are regulation and co-ordination. Regulatory functions include safari quotas and other consumptive use of wildlife, licensing, prosecution of offenders against the Wildlife Act, gazettement of wildlife areas and supervision of photographic tourism in their areas. TANAPA is responsible for the management, conservation and use of all national parks in Tanzania. TANAPA is a parastatal and corporate body under a Board of Trustees; it provides guide services, promotes community conservation activities, and controls poaching in the national parks.

The utilization of wildlife resources through the consumptive trophy hunting industry and non-consumptive game viewing ("safari" tourism) are the two most important sources of wildlife related income in the Tanzanian economy. Other wildlife-based activities are, with the exception of capture and trade of live animals, under-developed in Tanzania. These include trade in bushmeat, skins and other products such as biltong, and farming of specific wildlife species. These products could offer potential growth opportunities, but markets, production facilities and the necessary policy framework do not presently support expansion of these activities.

Revenue generated from wildlife resources accrues to the MNRT mainly from hunting licenses; such licenses generated more than TSh9 million during 2004. In addition, about US$30 million was generated from tourists' hunting, and US$9 million was generated by private companies that lease hunting concessions from the government. In 2002, earnings from live animal exports amounted to roughly US$170,000. In aggregate, the direct contribution by the sector is just under 1 percent of GDP.

Tourism

One of the largest income earners in the country is the non-consumptive use of wildlife resources: game viewing by international tourists. Tanzania boasts some of the world's finest tourist attractions, notably the Serengeti National Park and the Ngorongoro Wildlife Conservation Area. In addition, as described above, the country has a notable income from hunting tourism. The National Tourism Policy stresses wildlife conservation, due to the fact that Tanzania's tourism is largely wildlife based. It states that "... the government vows to ... improve and implement wildlife conservation regulations, and to protect other tourist attractions for the benefits of present and future generations." While MNRT and TANAPA remain the lead agencies associated with tourism development, the tourism sector has also benefited greatly from the increased openness of the economy and the influx of foreign investment. The private sector has provided a significant boost to this sector, with increased provision of services and employment opportunities. The sector currently provides an estimated 200,000 jobs, although seasonally fluctuations can be considerable.

Tourist visits and contribution to GDP peaked in the late 1990s, at over 600,000 visitors; short-term declines thereafter are largely attributed to security concerns from the U.S. Embassy bombings in 1998 in Dar es Salaam and in Nairobi, and through general global travel insecurity after the September 11 attacks in the United States in 2001. In 2001, Tanzanian national parks drew more than 100,000 international visitors and this tourism generated receipts of almost 5 percent of GDP, equivalent to about US$400 million. Visitation statistics for the country as a whole in 2004 show 582,000 visitors, although GDP contribution has fallen because of the strength of other sectors.

It is important to note that cultural monuments, archives and antiquities currently attract around 60,000 tourists per year, with more than 90 percent of the visitors coming from abroad. The most frequented site is Olduvai Gorge, attracting almost 90 percent of all visitors. Recent data suggest that the collection of fees is rising; collected fees increased from TSh96 million in 2002 to approximately TSh133 million in 2003.

Mining

In strictly economic terms, mineral resources are probably the most important natural resource in Tanzania. In recent years, the mineral industry has produced copper, gold, silver, and rolled steel products, and such industrial minerals as calcite, diamond and other gemstones, gypsum, phosphate rock, salt, silica sand, and soda ash. Deposits of cobalt, copper, iron ore, natural gas, nickel, and titanium are also known to occur in Tanzania. The sector is characterized by a concentration of large scale mines (mainly gold and diamonds) and a diversity of small scale operators in the artisanal mining sector.

The Mining sector in Tanzania mainland grew by 27.4 percent in 1998 as a reflection of massive foreign investment in the large-scale mining sector. In subsequent years, growth has been lower, but still remained double digit. The growth in the sector reflects a significant increase in the annual production of gold in the large-scale sector that has, following the liberalization of the sector in the late 1990s, increased to a level of more than 45,000 kg in 2003. Yet, mining is a small sector; it accounts for about 3.5 percent of GDP (2005). Hence, despite its rapid growth, general GDP growth has not been significantly affected by the growth in the sector.

The state monopoly of the mining industry of the 1970s ended in the late 1980s opening the way for any citizen to register claims and sell minerals. In consequence, the number of small-scale miners grew rapidly. The growth was further boosted in the early 1990s with the government permitting exporters to use their proceeds for financing imported goods, equipment and spare parts. Consequently, the number of people employed in small-scale mining operations surpassed 500,000 by 1995. Current estimates of artisanal mining place employment figures as high as 1 million but precise numbers are not known because of the difficulty in monitoring and registering activity. In contrast, the large scale mining is estimated to employ about 30,000 workers.

Mining in Tanzania is governed by the Mining Act (1998), which is overseen by the Ministry of Energy and Minerals (MEM), and is administered by the Mineral Resources Department (MRD). The Bank of Tanzania buys the minerals from licensed miners and dealers. In mining areas, Regional and District Administrations provide social services and settle disputes between local community, individuals, claim holders or mining companies. Environmental issues governing the sector are overseen by NEMC, with proponents responsible for mine reclamation activities. Since trade liberalization, various mining associations have formed: REMA and FEMATA unite small-scale miners at, respectively, regional and national levels; TAMIDA brings together gem miners and brokers; TAWOMA represents women miners; and the Chamber of Mines protects the interests of small- and large-scale miners, and mining companies. Recently, significant effort has been dedicated to reviewing and potentially amending various fiscal and tax instruments that govern the sector; some mining operations are grandfathered under historical tax regimes while new activities are generally governed by provisions that treat the sector more akin to typical commercial investments with no specialized provisions. Most analysts concur that the nature of distortions in the large-scale mining sector are quite limited, with the sector performing well overall; but there does remain some concern that exploration activity is inadequate to guarantee the sector's future. In the artisanal and small-scale sector, there are significant weaknesses that contribute to economic losses and social disruptions. Within the citizenry as a whole there is a widespread perception that mining revenues are not benefiting the common person.

Counting the Unaccounted: Some Methodological Background

Although natural resource assets, like labor and capital, contribute to the economy and the subsistence base of the rural population, their value and potential is underestimated. This underestimation is partly based on missing markets for public goods, imperfect competition, distortion by government interventions, and pricing of natural resources below market value. The result of all these market failures leads to suboptimal economic decisionmaking and loss of income to the country.

Also, because of weak governance regimes in revenue-generating sectors, resources are often offered below market price to the benefit of a few powerful winners and to the loss of the majority of the rural population. Yet, these natural resources provide substantive potential for income to communities in rural areas. For example, the weaknesses in governance regimes in forestry, wildlife, and fisheries include: (a) a lack of transparency and accountability in issuing rights to extract resources and accrue revenues from them, (b) inequitable sharing of benefits with communities, and (c) weak monitoring and surveillance of stocks. In the principal sectors providing natural capital in the growth equation (forestry, wildlife, fisheries, and mining) royalties are set arbitrarily and do not reflect scarcity. Royalties are, hence, not used as a policy instrument of intertemporal resource pricing and sustained yield management. As long as these weaknesses are not addressed, a substantial base of economic growth will slowly erode and poverty reduction objectives are unlikely to be achieved.

To draw attention to the scale of this hidden economy, we rely on some increasingly standardized methods for accounting for such losses. In many instances, these losses are real—they are values that do not accrue to the benefit of Tanzanians, while in other cases they are simply not reflected in national accounts or standard monitoring methods. At this stage, it is thus useful to review briefly some of these issues methods.

We start by considering four quite separate issues within the context of how natural resources contribute to or are influenced by economic development: (i) the natural resource curse; (ii) macroeconomic effects on natural resource quality; (iii) the role of the poor; and (iv) precaution and environmental vulnerability.[2]

---

2. The first three of these issues draw partially from COWI (2005) Volume 1.

The Natural Resource Curse: Natural Resources as an Economic Drag

The point of departure here is the so-called resource curse hypothesis, arguing that countries with an abundance of natural resources will have lower growth rates as the more productive manufacturing sector is crowded out. Empirical evidence generally supports the existence of such linkages, even though the exact mechanism is not always clear. In Tanzania's case, however, there is no direct evidence of such an economic drag occurring. The natural resource sectors that would be theoretically most prone to this are large scale mining (because of the large income generation) and agriculture (because of the large labor force that is not released to more productive manufacturing endeavours). In the mining sector, however, most investment was associated with specialized foreign inflows and there was likely no direct crowding out effect. With land and agriculture production, there is still insufficient evidence to suggest that the terms of trade have been drastically affected to suspect that this effect may be at work. In brief, natural resources are likely to play a continued positive contribution to national output.

Income as Curse or Cure: The Environmental Kuznets Curve

The key issue here is whether general economic growth will have positive or negative impacts on the resource base. As countries get richer, the increased consumption places increased pressure on scarce resources. Industrial production requires water, for instance, and increased output is often gained at the expense of land and water quality degradation. More intensive agricultural production—through the use of pesticides or fertilizers—may also have negative impacts on resource quality. There is evidence that such issues are important within Tanzania. The other end of the equation is that, at some stage, the income also becomes a potential cure to the natural resource and environmental degradation. Increased income permits increased investment in environmentally appropriate infrastructure, it allows financing of institutions tasked with maintaining environmental standards, it permits financing of educational and training initiatives that promote sustainable resource use and management. The resultant curve—the "Environmental Kuznets Curve (EKC)"— generally asserts that increased income will initially threaten some resources but will eventually provide a means for protecting the natural resource base. This EKC is by no means a straightforward relationship, but illustrates the linkages that are known to exist between development and natural resource quality. Such linkages are evident in Tanzania, and provide important feedback opportunities in resource management.

The Poor: Culprits or Victims

Associated with the EKC is the role of the poor within the overall linkage structure. Some assert that the poor cause resource degradation because their plight requires that they think for the short term and do not have the luxury of long-term planning that may be necessary for renewable resource planning. Others assert that the poor are more typically victims of inequitable participation models and suffer from resource degradation that is not their own doing. Both instances can be documented in Tanzania; poverty near wildlife reserves and parks has resulted in non-sustainable poaching by the poor in some areas. In coastal areas, the poor are adversely affected by illegal dynamite fishing, which is typically practiced by richer fishermen with access to more sophisticated equipment and materials. In reality, management interventions must be capable of addressing all such situations to ensure that resources are managed in a sustainable manner; such interventions always require some degree of support for more equitable participation in resource revenues and management decisionmaking.

Precautionary Linkages

The issue of precaution is directly linked to uncertainty. Unlike quantifiable risks, the notion of "uncertainty" is that there is no basis for knowing the likelihood or probability of some outcome or event. Events are so rare, or with so little precedent, that traditional methods of risk management may not be appropriate. The "precautionary principle" therefore asserts that one should adopt management strategies that are capable of protecting core values irrespective of the costs of such strategies; the standard benefit:cost metric does not apply, and the idea of cost-effectiveness—looking for a protective strategy that gives an adequate safety net—is more appropriate. Policymakers have experience with such measures; military spending, certain healthcare interventions, and measures that protect core ecosystems such as water supplies fall within this category. Environmental vulnerability can be treated similarly. Indeed, Tanzania's resource development strategy cited earlier (that calls for avoiding extinction of any given renewable resource) captures the spirit of precautionary measures. From an accounting perspective, the nature of uncertainty is that no values can be placed on being precautionary, but lessons from elsewhere and Tanzania dictate that attention needs to be paid to ensure that options remain open to future generations.

Capturing these linkages in appropriate management mechanisms is by no means trivial. A first step is often to describe the values associated with such linkages, and with the parts of economic production that may be lost or hidden because of various effects within this complex system. Methods of green accounting, resource valuation, and assessments of externalities have contributed a great deal to improving our understanding of these linkages. The discussion below shows how some of these methods can be applied to estimating the size of the hidden economy within Tanzania.

The Hidden Economy Revealed

Much has been written on the "informal," "illegal," "casual," "second," "cash," "parallel," "underground," or "subsistence" economy. In general, these writings refer to production that does not move through documented markets, but that may have value to the economy as a whole. This hidden economy is not just a feature of developing countries, but the scale of the hidden economy tends to be larger where markets are less well developed and where administrative structures for monitoring them are weaker. In 2000, for example, surveys estimated that the hidden economy in OECD countries represented 18 percent of production while in developing countries it approached 41 percent of GNI (Schneider 2002). At the time of the survey of 110 countries, Tanzania (along with Nigeria and Zimbabwe) had among the largest informal economies documented; the scale of Tanzania's informal economy stood at 58.3 percent of formal GNI at the time. It should therefore come as no surprise that, during the review of various sectoral activities, significant unaccounted production values were identified in major sectors.

Within the context of this paper, it is important to note that production within this hidden economy is not necessarily "lost" output. Even illegal activities can have positive implications for economic output if the benefits of the activity are retained within the economy. The downside of those activities is often distributional, either because they involve a loss to treasury or uncompensated losses to certain individuals or groups within the country. The cases we will generally describe in this paper distinguish among different types of hidden economy:

- Those having positive impacts on domestic production, but creating inequities or inefficiencies in resource development. Domestic fisheries and wildlife consumption may fall within this category.
- Those associated with lost opportunities because of economic leakages, creating inequities and inefficiencies in resource development. Incorrect resource pricing within the marine fishery sector, for example, can lead to this situation.
- Those that create negative externalities domestically, irrespective of whether their direct production impacts are hidden. An example of this is the tourism sector, where in some places carrying capacity has been reached or exceeded.

Fisheries

A great share of the marine catch does not enter GDP and export statistics but plays an important role in livelihood support. In the offshore, the official number of artisanal fishermen has doubled since 1995, reaching close to 120,000 in 2003. Some of the consumption, involving dynamite fishing in reef areas, is clearly illegal. In freshwater fisheries, some 200,000 fishermen are involved in the sector, with that production not captured within official statistics. In aggregate, the value of this own consumption is of the order of 2 to 4 percent of GDP annually.

While the own-consumption is not lost to the economy, unsustainable harvesting and externalities associated with marine and offshore fisheries do reflect an economic loss. Much of the rents from offshore fisheries are not captured because of inefficient licensing regimes, and an inability to monitor and enforce catch within the EEZ. Historically boats have not been properly licensed, and it is only recently that more effort has been placed on licensing and monitoring of catch. Even so, the license fees associated with the foreign fishing likely reflect an order of magnitude loss of revenues. Implementation of the DSFA is intended to improve this situation.

Forestry

The difficulty of examining Forestry in the context of economic growth arises because no markets exist for many of the sector's contributions to the Tanzanian economy. Hence, there is no objectively verifiable monetary value in which these services could be measured. Water services, biodiversity, climate regulation, and cultural values are examples of such forest services. Although these ecosystem functions of forests can be determinants to growth in other sectors, via the water and energy supply chain, these values are usually not reflected in the GDP. Many transactions related to forest products and services, although markets exists, fall within the informal sector or are undertaken illegally and hence are not recorded either. These are for example, the sale of non-timber forest products or illegal logging for timber and charcoal production. Official GDP figures do not reflect the true economic importance of the forest sector to the national economy.

Unaccounted-for services and non-industrial forestry reach 10 to 15 percent of GDP. This is equivalent to an annual increment of US$35 to US$50 per capita in income to every person in Tanzania. Forests provide about 75 percent of building materials and 100 percent of indigenous medicinal plants and supplementary food products. In addition, forests provide an important component of value added to national income through their ecosystem service functions, providing for industrial and domestic water and energy supply. Some 95 percent of Tanzania's energy consumption is in the form of fuelwood—consumption that is a major input factor for rural industries such as tobacco curing and fish smoking. Forests provide watershed functions for major rivers feeding into the national hydropower dams. The lack of reliable power and water supplies can hamper growth in the long term and is already being cited as a serious constraint in attracting private investment.

Wildlife

In addition to its direct use in trophy hunting and in game viewing, wildlife provides unaccounted-for subsistence values. Well over two-thirds of the people eat wild game, with up to 95 percent of the rural population claiming it as their most important meat protein source. In addition, the sector remains characterized by leakages through illegal trade, lack of transparency and non-implementation of government policies. Losses associated with the sector are difficult to estimate, as the primary consequences are distributional in nature. For example, while regulations require devolution of authority to village or local authorities, centralized structures persist and favor existing concessionaires.

Tourism

Private sector involvement in tourism has nurtured competitiveness and expanded the tourism product. The leakages that remain are more often associated with missed opportunities for developing local spin-offs. Studies have shown, for example, that the spin-offs and revenue retention from budget tourism is considerable greater than it is for the high end tourism that has persisted in many of Tanzania's traditional tourist circuits. Zanzibar is also re-orienting its tourism policies to capture some of the potential value-added from longer-stay tourists.

A second type of loss associated with tourism is that arising from potential negative externalities that are not adequately reflected in the pricing of other resources. For example, some tourist areas are now regarded as having reached their carrying capacity and rationing systems could be used to reduce pressures and increase the revenue potential from those assets. This is particularly true for areas (such as coasts and undeveloped areas) over which property and use rights have not yet been established.

Mining

Whereas the revenues of large-scale mining operations are scrutinized for tax purposes, most of the income of artisanal and small-scale mining (ASM) is in the hidden economy. An estimated 90 percent of some 550,000 miners (1995) are unlicensed and hence non-reporting. Data on ASM activity are consequently scarce, as are data on mineral brokers and dealers. In 1998, the year before large-scale exports were reported, the Ministry of Energy and Minerals (MEM) reported precious metals exports, which would have been attributed wholly to ASM, to be about US$22 million. For that same year, a study that accounted for smuggled minerals estimated the real value to be US$136 million, about six times greater than that reported (Phillips and others 2001a). Other estimates of the value of gold smuggling alone vary between US$45 million and US$200 million.

Reported mineral exports for 2002/03 were in the order of US$623 million for which some US$38 million in revenue was collected by government through royalties, corporate income tax, and various withholding taxes. The bulk of those exports were from large-scale, capital intensive operations that employ relatively few miners (some 30,000), and import most of their equipment. By contrast, small-scale operations employ hundreds of thousands of workers, whose informal activities could be bringing revenue into their communities that rivals the amounts currently being collected though royalties and taxes.

Despite the reportedly high level of mineral smuggling, it is estimated that more than 70 percent of the export value of the minerals remains in Tanzania. Most of the value added to the mineral commodities is in the mining and the marketing, and these are mostly Tanzanian operators, who in turn inject this hidden cash into the local rural economies. If 70 percent of the smuggled value remains in the country, given the above conjectured value of gold smuggling, small-scale miners could be injecting between US$32 million and US$140 million into their communities. Despite the lack of official data, it is clear that ASM has contributed significantly to local economies, albeit informally.

Carbon Resources

Ten years ago carbon resources were not generally regarded as a tradable commodity. As a consequence of the Kyoto Protocol, trade in services from these resources is now emerging. The protocol was negotiated in 1997 as part of the United Nations Framework Convention on Climate Change and formally came into effect in February 2005. To offset the effects of greenhouse gases (GHG) on overall climate change, markets have emerged that permit countries or industries to trade in "emission reductions (ERs)" that can be verified and certified as incremental reductions in GHG emissions. If a country such as Tanzania can demonstrably generate such ERs, then they have a tradable export commodity that earns hard foreign exchange. Methodologies for assigning values and certifying ERs are being developed on a continuous basis, but a wide variety of projects are already capturing some benefit from this mechanism. Tree planting generates ERs because growing trees absorb and sequester carbon dioxide. Composting of municipal organic wastes generates ERs because it avoids the eventual production of methane (a GHG with 25 times the negative impact as carbon dioxide) when such wastes decompose under anaerobic conditions in landfills. The flaring of methane from petroleum production can generate ERs if that gas would otherwise have been vented openly. At present, no mature projects have been developed within Tanzania, but the focal point for such activities is at a high political level—within the Vice President's Office of the Government.

The value of the country's carbon resources is not readily estimated. To place it in perspective, however, it suffices to consider the value associated with the existing mature forests in the country as well as with newly planted forests; a growing forest sequesters carbon more rapidly than a mature forest and thus has a different value. The asset value of carbon sequestration services provided by Tanzania's standing forests is estimated to be between US$700 and US$1,500 per hectare; for the 33.5 million ha forest estate as a whole, this translates to a minimum asset value of US$24 billion. Newly planted forests or plantations would add to this asset value through generating new ERs; such plantations in Uganda have recently captured the equivalent of US$50 per hectare annually for a plantation growth cycle of some eleven years.[3] These carbon values are of the same order of magnitude as the commercial timber value and payments streams can contribute meaningfully to sustainable management of the forest; the payments also provide a means for providing ongoing service payments to local communities that assist in forest management.

Water

Water does not directly enter into Tanzania's GDP accounts, but Tanzania's economic performance is very dependent on access to water. The 2003 GDP growth rate of 5.6 percent was less than the projected rate of 6.5 percent largely because of the impact that drought had on the agriculture, manufacturing, livestock, and energy sectors. Regionally for 2006, growth projections for East Africa are being downgraded as water shortages contribute to crop failures, power outages, and livestock losses. The consumptive uses of water are manifold, and all contribute to social well-being or improved economic output: within the Tanzania Water Resources Assistance Strategy (TWRAS), a distinction is made among various overarching goals that include: (i) water for people; (ii) water for food; (iii) water for energy; (iv) water for environment; and, (v) water for other uses.

This report suggests (in Chapter 4) that water itself can be seen as an overarching theme for addressing some of the broader protection and safety-net issues that are required within a coherent natural resource management strategy. This is because of its multiple linkages to other key sectors, and the vulnerability of these sectors to inadequate water quality or quantity. The agriculture sector, 48 percent of Tanzania's GDP, is primarily rainfed and susceptible to drought while most irrigated agriculture is along watercourses with little scope for headwater storage. Small-scale irrigators have no secure tenure over water rights. Water supply for livestock is unreliable and is often diverted to other uses. In the energy sector, about 70 percent of Tanzania's power is hydroelectric and is vulnerable to illegal upstream water abstraction and poor enforcement of water rights. Contamination of waterways and lakes directly impacts the quality of fisheries, which are an important source of protein and also contribute to the country's export earnings. Tourism, mining, and wildlife all require water as a critical input.

---

3. The Rwoho Central Forest Reserve area being replanted consists of 2,137 ha of mixed forest that will generate approximately 260,000 tons of carbon dioxide ERs over a period of eleven years. These ERs were valued at slightly over US$4/t CO_2 in mid-2006.

The government has taken a number of significant steps to try to modernize governance and management of this key resource. Following a series of crises in the early 1990s, the URT fundamentally changed the way it managed the basic water resource. A new Water Policy was approved in 2002 involving a phased transfer of responsibility for operational matters to river basin level, restructuring of the central agency to remove duplication and inefficiencies, greater involvement of stakeholders in decisions, greater private sector involvement in major water supply and sanitation (WSS) operations, and introduction of charges for water use and licenses for water pollution. In addition, the URT focused attention on the management of its priority river basins and three lake basins, and become more involved in cooperative management with neighboring countries of its transboundary regional lakes and rivers. Further reforms to address sectoral weaknesses remain key priorities of government and development partners.[4]

Characterizing the Weaknesses and Potential Responses

The Weaknesses: Governance, Inefficiency and Vulnerability

While the general weaknesses within the sector may be associated with various policy failures, addressing such weaknesses requires very specific interventions and responses. A diagnostic framework is thus developed here to permit a synthesis of the major weaknesses, and some ranking of their relative magnitude. Actual examples will be developed throughout this paper, but at this stage it is instructive to show a summary of the general areas requiring policy responses.

We distinguish among three general types of weaknesses. First, those associated with *poor governance* are typically caused by a range of institutional failures that contribute to corrupt or illegal practices. In its simplest form, the failure can be the lack of an effective and responsible organization to oversee the activity; forestry, wildlife, and artisanal mining all suffer to varying degrees from this weakness. Carbon resources also lack an effective central organizing structure, but that is largely because the newness of the activity. Another contributor to poor governance is a lack of transparency in how administrative matters are handled; this lack of transparency and accountability may or may not be directly related to corruption, but corruption is often assumed and thus influences overall behaviour in the sector. The prevalence of persistent illegal activities is also characteristic of overall poor governance. The sectors addressed in this study suffer to varying degrees from these indicators of poor governance. Tourism, large-scale mining, and freshwater fisheries probably require the fewest corrections in this area, while forestry and artisanal mining would be high priorities in any reform agenda.

The second type of weakness is what we describe as overall *inefficiency* in resource management, usually in an economic sense. These are associated with various market failures that can usually be corrected through adequate market-based interventions. Such market-based interventions may also need to be supported by some institutional strengthening, but the institutional strengthening is fundamentally of a different type than that required

---

4. The recently adopted Water Resources Assistance Strategy (World Bank 2006) provides a comprehensive plan for addressing these weaknesses and is regarded as a key element to the protection of the natural resource sector as a whole.

Table 1.3. Synopsis of Sectoral Weaknesses, Incidence, and Corrective Options

Weakness →		Poor Governance	Inefficiency	Vulnerability
General Examples		No Responsible Institution (R) Lack of Transparency (T) Illegal Activities (I)	No Property Right Clarity (PR) Incorrect Resource Pricing (P) Distorting Subsidies/Taxes (D) Unfair Distribution (U)	Ecosystem Vulnerability (E) Social Vulnerability (S) Limited Diversification (D) Other External Shocks (O)
Scale or Prevalence	Fisheries (freshwater)	None/Limited	Moderate (P + U)	Extensive (E + S + D + O)
	Fisheries (marine)	Moderate (T)	Extensive (PR + P + D + U)	Extensive (E + S + O)
	Forestry	Moderate(R)	Moderate (PR + P)	Moderate (E + S)
	Wildlife	Moderate (R + T + I)	Extensive (PR + P + D + U)	Moderate (E + S)
	Tourism	None/Limited	Limited/Moderate (U)	Moderate (E + S + O)
	Mining (large-scale)	None/Limited	Limited/Moderate (D + U)	None/Limited (O)
	Mining (artisanal)	Extensive (R + T + I)	Extensive (PR + P + U)	Moderate (S + O)
	Carbon Resources	Limited (R)	Moderate (PR)	Moderate (S + O)
	Water (consumptive)	Moderate (R)	Moderate (PR + P)	Extensive (E + S + D + O)
Corrective Options		Institutional Reforms Training Improved Transparency & Monitoring	Property Right Reforms Resource Pricing Tax/Subsidy Reform Institutional Restructuring	Revenue Retention Co-management Education & Awareness Vulnerability Monitoring Diversification

to correct poor governance. In Table 1.3, we distinguish among four different contributors to inefficiency. First, lack of property rights, or lack of clarity in property rights, may lead to open access extraction or to resource use conflicts that create other management problems. Property right regimes remain weakest in the areas of forestry, wildlife, and offshore fishery resources. Even where property rights may be well-defined and respected, improper resource pricing can cause sub-optimal extraction or development of the asset. Inappropriate or non-existent use of regulatory instruments (such as leases or royalties) are examples of this pricing failure. A third type of inefficiency can arise from taxation or subsidy systems; such distortions can be at a project level (through inappropriate subsidies or taxes) or can be macro-economic in nature (such as through export or import policies that distort incentive structures). Finally, a fourth but significant contributor to inefficiency is the perceived fairness of management arrangements (either in revenue sharing, employment opportunities, or decisionmaking authority). This last area of "fair distribution" is often treated as a separate policy objective but we treat it here as a necessary and important component of overall resource management efficiency. There is ample evidence that such inequities themselves lead to conflicts, theft, and higher administrative costs associated with monitoring and compliance systems; fair systems are thus more efficient systems in the long term.

The third type of weakness we characterize as *vulnerability*, and it deserves a separate style of intervention. Traditional interventions often focused on correcting just governance and market failures, but such corrections do not necessarily recognize that some sectors and activities are intrinsically more vulnerable than others. Within an overall complex economic system, this may be critical for stability as a whole if the scale of such vulnerabilities becomes significant. It is important to note that many vulnerabilities are *intrinsic* to the type of activity, the vulnerabilities themselves can not necessarily be eliminated. What may be possible is to reduce the effects of such vulnerability. In this context, we distinguish between the following four types of vulnerability. First, ecosystem vulnerability is a characteristic of certain habitats and systems that may be approaching critical thresholds in terms of extent, quality, or character. For example, mangroves—which are specifically protected in legislation and overseen by competent management authorities—are nonetheless vulnerable in many areas of the country because they were historically overexploited and have not yet recovered. Second, social vulnerability of the affected populations and communities is a contributing force to overall instability. Activities that involve the poor are inherently more vulnerable than others. A third contributor to overall vulnerability is the lack of diversification opportunities within an activity; artisanal gold mining is an example of this. Finally, there exists a large array of "other" influences in the form of stochastic external shocks over which an activity may have no control. Some sectors (such as tourism) are more prone to these than others, based on historical experiences. Protection of water resources, as discussed previously, is a multi-sectoral priority that can serve as a basis for addressing vulnerability issues throughout the economy.

An Agenda for Action: Reform, Management, and Protection

The corrective intervention options in each of these three areas correspond directly to the underlying problems. We characterize these broadly as governance reforms, management interventions, and protection interventions. The governance reforms are intended to strengthen governance regimes through training, institutional reforms and mechanisms that improve transparency and monitoring systems. Management interventions improve the efficiency of natural resource use through property right reforms, adjustments to resource pricing instruments or levels, changes to tax and subsidy regimes, and supportive institutional restructuring. Interventions that perform a safety net function include a wide variety of instruments, including some that are intended specifically to address equity issues and social vulnerability. These safety net options include: implementation of revenue retention schemes; promotion of explicit co-management models that involve local, national and regional participants; investments in education and awareness building; enhanced vulnerability monitoring; and, investments that increase diversification opportunities. It should be noted that these distinctions are made to facilitate identification of priority areas and to provide a clear classification of the intent of various interventions. The concepts and interventions are elaborated in the following chapters, providing specific recommendations within each sector.

CHAPTER 2

Reform: Striking Down Corruption and Illegal Activities

The Business Case for Reducing Corruption

The first pillar—reform—focuses squarely on eliminating corruption and improving transparency. We start here because, in the absence of a good governance regime, other interventions intended to promote efficient resource use or to provide backstop safety-nets will not work. An administratively and economically efficient royalty and taxation regime will be of no help if gold and diamonds are being stolen or illegally smuggled. A safety-net scheme to distribute food or water to drought-stricken areas is of no use if the goods are diverted to black markets that benefit a handful of people while further impoverishing others.

While in some circles corruption is regarded as a tolerable cultural phenomenon, there is increasing evidence that poor governance directly affects an economy's performance. Recent research demonstrates that the process of development should be treated as total wealth management. Accordingly, national wealth is a portfolio containing three asset groups: natural capital (forests, land, fish), produced capital (infrastructure, factories), and intangible capital (skilled and unskilled labor, institutional quality). The financial return on these assets is today's and tomorrow's consumption possibilities and, hence, national well-being. To the extent that the portfolio's asset base is eroded and compensating investment is not undertaken, future returns—future consumption possibilities—decline.

Certain assets in the portfolio such as minerals are non-renewable, but they can be transformed into other forms of productive assets (infrastructure, human capital), if resource rents are captured and invested. Renewable natural resource assets can yield a sustainable return, if incentives and institutions promote their sustainable use. Produced capital assets depreciate, requiring on-going investment in maintenance and replacement, while intangible capital assets require nurturing in the form of investment in education, institutional quality, and good governance. Productive investment in one form or another maintains or increases total wealth.

Total wealth estimates show that in most countries natural and produced capital account for the smallest fractions of total wealth. In fact, most of a country's wealth is intangible capital; as income increases, the share of natural resources in total wealth declines, while the share of intangible capital increases. Intangible capital is composed of human capital (skills and know-how of the labor force), social capital (trust among citizens and their ability to work together for common goals), and governance. Governance encompasses those elements that boost the productivity of the economy. If an economy has an efficient judicial system, clear property rights, and effective government, the effects will be higher total wealth and increased intangible capital.[5] Intangible capital feeds itself and increases the likelihood that productive investment is undertaken for the natural and produced capital assets.

Given the importance of intangible capital in total wealth management, it is useful to understand the factors that affect it. Education is of course a key factor. The other very important factor is institutional quality. It is described to include governance dimensions of voice and accountability, political stability and absence of violence, government effectiveness, regulatory quality, rule of law, and control of corruption.

Data analyses in a recent World Bank (2006b) report use school years per capita to capture education levels, and a rule of law index to capture institutional quality. The rule of law is a proxy for overall institutional quality, because it measures the extent to which people have confidence in, and abide by, the rules of society. Regression analysis using international data showed that the rule of law had the greatest effect on intangible capital: a 1 percent increase in it would boost intangible capital by 0.83 percent. The same increase in schooling would boost it by 0.53 percent.

In Tanzania, significant progress has been made nation-wide in improving governance conditions. Diagnostic indicators compiled for Tanzania by the World Bank Institute are shown in Figure 2.1. Over the seven-year period from 1998 to 2005, governance has improved in terms of voice and accountability, government effectiveness, and the control of corruption. Improvements in the control of corruption have been particularly impressive. The discussion below summarizes high priority outstanding issues in the sectors we are addressing in this report, as well as providing positive examples of reforms that have been done. We conclude with recommended priority reform actions.

Reducing corruption and improving governance conditions requires, foremost, political will. There is substantial evidence of such political will at the highest levels in Tanzania. A new anti-corruption bill was put forward to parliament in early 2007 that incorporates many of the best practices of existing international and regional anti-corruption legislation. In the presence of such political will, it is possible to eliminate illegal activities, improve accountability, and enhance the information base for monitoring and compliance. This is achieved through specific potential interventions related to training, institutional capacity building and reform, and improved transparency within decisionmaking and monitoring mechanisms.[6]

---

5. Intangible capital is measured as the residual after produced and natural resources have been deducted from total wealth.

6. The World Bank supports a wide range of programs to improve governance that includes these kinds of interventions. Such interventions were the topic of commitments made at the recent meetings in Singapore (September 2006). In addition, judicial reforms are frequently cited as a necessary means for improving governance but these are de-emphasized for Tanzania and not treated in this paper.

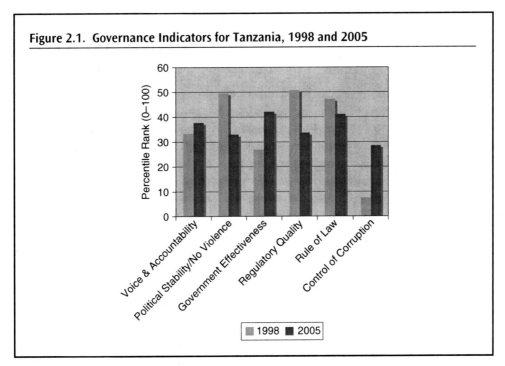

Figure 2.1. Governance Indicators for Tanzania, 1998 and 2005

Source: World Bank Institute (2006).

The Need for Reform: Sectoral Overview

Chapter 1 provided some initial indication of weaknesses across all sectors but here we elaborate more fully on those sectors with the greatest lapses. We note that the freshwater fisheries, tourism, and large-scale mining sectors suffer from few serious governance issues and these sectors are therefore de-emphasized here. These sectors are, however, still prone to various management and vulnerability issues that will be addressed in subsequent chapters.

Fisheries (Marine)

Governance issues in the marine sector of fisheries are not that pervasive, and revolve primarily around transparency and accountability issues in the delivery of licenses and around illegal fishing in territorial waters. The latter poses a risk to fish and prawn stocks while also damaging fragile ecosystems and protected areas because of the techniques being used. The transparency weaknesses are associated with differences in fee levels and regimes between Zanzibar and the mainland, both of which license vessels to fish in the marine waters. The illegal fishing is linked to this, and exacerbated by lack of coordinating bodies with adequate capacity to monitor and enforce compliance. It is anticipated that many of the underlying offshore institutional issues will be addressed when the Deep Sea Fishing Authority (DSFA) becomes operational in 2007.

One international governance issue that remains outstanding is the lack of a formal agreement between URT and Comoros relating to the boundary of the EEZ. Both countries have defined the identical EEZ limit (based on the equidistance principle) in their domestic legislation, hence there is no overlap or uncertainty regarding the boundary, but the bilateral agreements that cover recognition and management of the boundary have not yet been signed.

Forestry

Poor governance in the forestry sector has been pervasive for some time and, while the government has made some positive steps and commitments to sectoral reform, many weaknesses persist. Many of the institutional issues are associated with the administrative settings, which provide opportunities for corruption that build on weak accounting systems. Revenue collection systems are weak and the sector has yet to rid itself of perceptions that revenue leakages may be associated with such corruption.

The major conflicts in the sector arise from weak administrative arrangements and the lack of clear authorities. Under the current administrative setting within local government, district forest staff are answerable to the District Executive Directors while issues associated with accountability and transparency are typically referred back to DFOB. The conflicts that arise under such an arrangement have resulted in ongoing discussions among DFOB and the local government authorities, with assistance from the President's Office (through PORALG). Ad hoc working groups attempt to resolve the issues but the outcomes of such efforts often appear as arbitrary decisions.

The multiple levels of responsibility have also resulted in lapses in accounting. Forest assets are not included in the national accounts and no reliable national database of forest inventory exists.

Wildlife

Governance weaknesses in the wildlife sector are reflected by various incidents that show weaknesses in administration and unclear responsibilities among institutional players. Part of this is because of historical administrative divisions, such as different roles of Wildlife Division and TANAPA, while some is because of the government's own policy that seeks to devolve some management to local authorities or to the private sector. The resultant transitions have often resulted in non-transparent systems, unresolved conflicts, and—at times—illegal activities or cases that cannot be successfully prosecuted. Corrective actions for many of these institutional problems are underway, but there is ample scope for continued institutional strengthening and training.

A non-transparent system of quota setting for the hunting industry by government has historically resulted in imperfect competition in the market, and current structures have not in most cases progressed beyond this point. There is no competitive tendering for hunting concessions but distribution through autonomous government decisionmaking. Effective market forces are hence not applied to optimize revenues. This policy intervention resulted in a monopoly of knowledge by the Wildlife Division and an oligopsony in terms of access to the resource, a situation in which a small number of large buyers controls the market. Consequently, quotas are sold below market value leading to a loss in revenue. While imperfect competition usually benefits a few powerful players, it is at the disadvantage to the majority of the population. It leads to loss of income and livelihoods for rural communities, and discourages entry into the market place by potential bidders. Government still maintains that the allocation system (devised using a Block Allocation Committee) provides an appropriate balance between social and economic needs, and that it in fact ensures greater access by Tanzanians. The system, however, is open to abuse and arbitrary judgment, and is a definite drag on foreign investment.

Poaching remains a problem in many areas, and is exacerbated by weak local governments that do not (historically) have the means to regulate or enforce such activities. By TANAPA's own estimates some 40,000 animals are poached annually in the Serengeti plains area. While the historical move to decentralization is appropriate, it has not always been backed up by adequate training and complementary institutional strengthening at the local level. This has made it easier for illegal trade also to make its way into the system. For example, illegal trade of ivory from Tanzania to the Middle East is estimated to have caused a US$200 million revenue loss through a single consignment of ivory from 40 slaughtered elephants, evaluating the value of those elephants with their trophy price. In this case, corruption is based on organized criminal networks involving the police and government officials. MNRT reports that over a five-year period, 3,704 kg of ivory in transit were intercepted and more than 700 guns impounded at various exit points. There is a well-organized criminal network of illicit trade out of Tanga port; while the illicit trade pays the porters only TSh50 000 and exposes them to great risks, it brings prosperity to the middlemen. One consignment weighing 800 kg was stuffed into 10 boxes labeled as horticultural produce. Since the consignments are usually under police escort, it is difficult to stop illicit traffickers. The losses can be regarded as either a loss in income (to the extent that it may at some point have been capturable as trophy income) or a degradation of the wealth asset of the nation (with knock-on effects in reduced tourism income).

Mining (Artisanal)

Although large-scale mining proceeds in a relatively orderly fashion, the small-scale mining sector has numerous cases of poor governance. Unregistered (and thus illegal) activities proliferate, smuggling is rampant, and there are few paper trails that permit proper audit or tracking of transactions. Government ascribes these problems to the nature of the small-scale operations, while operators cite corruption within government, and the overall administrative burden coupled with bureaucratic inefficiencies as causes for non-compliance. Given the economic importance of this activity, investments in improving governance are warranted.

Illegal mining by ASMs on concession areas held by large-scale operators has been a potential source of conflict since large-scale operations began. However, conflicts in gold mining are fewer than in gemstone mining. Various anecdotal evidence points to cases of unclear property rights and forceful removal of small-scale miners from concession areas, as well as absconded compensation payments made by large-scale operators to ASMs. Large-scale operators are also subject to problematic illegal mining activity when they have vacated and rehabilitated a mined-out area, only to have it degraded again by small-scale miners who do not understand why they cannot mine abandoned areas.

A 1995–96 study indicated that about 60 percent of gemstones and 70 to 85 percent of gold produced by ASMs was illegally exported out of the country. Estimates of the value of smuggled exports are impressive, ranging from US$45 million to US$200 million per year. Some 95 percent of smuggled minerals leave Tanzania by the north into Kenya, mainly Nairobi. According to the sellers, they export outside of the country for reasons of price and convenience. With regard to gold, sellers said there were too few licensed Tanzanian dealers; in 1999 there were 5 licensed gold dealers in the country, down from 25 in 1998. The dealers who try to register claim harassment by local tax officials, who overestimate the markups in the sector and overstate the tax obligations. As for gems, Nairobi has been known to offer better prices and convenience for two main reasons: dealers there pay no transaction taxes, and they have more capital than Tanzanian dealers, so they pay cash on the spot. Tanzanian dealers often buy on consignment, waiting until they are paid before paying their suppliers.

Carbon Resources

Governance issues within the "carbon resource sector" are relatively few, primarily because of the low volume of activity to date. This low volume can, however, be partially ascribed to a lack of responsible authorities and the required legislative and regulatory instruments to deal with these activities. Although there is a focal point for the CDM (the vice-president's office) the operational capacity to handle such transactions is not yet well developed in the country. Potential stakeholders in this activity include forestry interests (public, private and community), municipal authorities, and energy generators, yet no formal mechanisms exist for these to interact with each other, to engage with foreign buyers of emission reductions, or to seek training.

Reform Examples in Tanzania

As noted above, Tanzania has been making good progress on governance issues in aggregate, and some specific examples of initiatives are evident within the resource sector. These examples can be used as models of what is possible, while also demonstrating that some level of political will exists to correct identified weaknesses.

Institutional Reforms and Reduction of Illegal Activity

In the fisheries sector, Tanzania has had recent successes that have been assisted by various donor-funded programs. In particular, the EU-SADC program has contributed to improved monitoring, control and surveillance (MCS) systems for foreign fishing vessels. The MCS systems permit tracking and identification of vessels engaged in illegal activities, and has led to charges being laid and vessels being impounded. The MCS program, which remains in its infancy, has increased the incentives for vessels to register and is largely responsible for the documented increases in such registrations and licensing. Although the EU-funded project drew to a close in late 2005, the World Bank and GEF supported Marine and Coastal Environment Management Project (MACEMP) that became effective in December 2005 also provides continued support for MCS efforts.

Also in the fishery sector, a significant institutional reform that will be implemented by the URT is the operationalization of the DSFA. In mid-2006 the mainland and Zanzibar agreed to operational modalities for revenue sharing and licensing within the EEZ. Parliament endorsed these modalities in February 2007 through passing amendments to the DSFA Act (1998) and the DSFA is expeccetd to begin operations formally in 2007. The DSFA structure is not new—it is well defined in the DSFA Act—but the institution did not heretofore have operational capacity because of outstanding issues relating to revenue collection and sharing. With these issues resolved, the DSFA will be an important responsible institution capable of addressing many current governance weaknesses in the sector.

Recent restructuring efforts in forestry provide the legislative basis for improved governance. The 2002 Forest Act authorizes villages to sell timber from their own forest reserves, which has potential to provide a new and additional source of forest revenue, directly accruing to the communities. Such community based forest management has provided revenue to villages across Tanzania and has provided opportunities for increased local participation. In addition, a new executive agency is being established that involves the transformation of the Forest and Beekeeping Division in MNRT.

Training, Education, and Awareness-building

In fisheries, the government has had success in the past in reducing illegal near-shore dynamite fishing through the use of education and awareness-building activities. In many parts of the country, dynamiting had been eliminated through engaging village groups in discussions that eventually resulted in the turning over of illegal gear and dynamite, and identification of perpetrators. Over the past year, dynamiting has again resurfaced, especially in Tanga areas on the mainland and Pemba in the Zanzibar isles. Increased patrol efforts have been partially successful in stemming the activity.

In mining, the MRD has improved its provision of extension services to small-scale miners by bringing such services and demonstration plants to specific mining regions. Since 1998 there have been efforts to transform informal mining and marketing through closer cooperation between the government departments involved in mining activity: the MRD, Income Tax, Internal Revenue and Customs. In response to analyses of the size of the small-scale mining sector, and the linkages between smuggling and taxation, the MEM reduced taxes and prosecutorial pressure on small-scale miners. These incentives are intended to induce ASMs to register activities.

Transparency and Monitoring

Perhaps one of the most impressive concepts of improved transparency and monitoring is that inherent in the Tanzania Social Action Fund (TASAF). TASAF was initiated with World Bank support and is now a stand-alone institution within government that provides poverty alleviation grants throughout the country for a wide variety of activities. Income earning activities are now eligible (within TASAF 2) and such activities can be complementary to other infrastructure development activities; fisheries management, wildlife management, and cultural property works are eligible activities within the TASAF structure. The TASAF concept stands out as best practice in transparency because it is targeted to the poor and incorporates an extensive development communications program that makes groups throughout the country aware of all of their entitlements and of the actual level of expenditures on any given project or sub-project. Radio programs, regular newspaper advertisements, and other mechanisms communicate detailed accounting information on a regular basis, permitting anybody to track expenditures. This openness reduces incentives for corruption and directly permits affected groups to become involved in program implementation. As TASAF expands to more activities and regions in the country, its greatest challenge will likely be to enhance the transparency and monitoring even more by being flexible and adaptive in its management approach.

Recommended Priority Reform Actions

It is acknowledged that institutional interventions are often lengthy procedures that do not have immediate impacts. Some of the interventions below thus represent continuations of on-going exercises. A sector-by-sector list of key interventions is provided in the Appendix; the following summarizes the key recommendations.

Institutional reform remains a high priority item in Tanzania as such reforms provide the basis for efficient management and any required safety-net interventions. The key sectoral reforms identified are:

- ■ *Operationalization of the Deep Sea Fishing Authority.* The DSFA will provide the basic institutional mechanism for sound management of the EEZ and its associated fishery resource. The existence of the DSFA will improve opportunities for Tanzania to work with regional partners in enforcing international agreements. It will also provide an impetus for improved management of other (non-fishery) marine resources.
- ■ *Creation of an Executive Agency responsible for Forestry.* The current division of responsibility between Districts and Central government requires reform. Plans to create an executive agency should be accelerated.
- ■ Review of *institutional arrangements affecting Wildlife Division and TANAPA*, with a view to establishing a single responsible executive agency for the sector. Wildlife management is currently divided among Wildlife Division, TANAPA, local authorities and private sector players. Transparency is poor and no clear mechanism is available for providing effective oversight. A thorough institutional review of all institutions is warranted, resulting in recommendations that will lead to the establishment of an effective executive agency.
- ■ The lack of effective governance within the *artisanal mining sector* is a concern that has not yet been adequately addressed within government. No appropriate institutional model exists for reform, although increased private sector involvement is warranted. A capacity review of MEM and related government organizations should be undertaken with a view to identifying appropriate training needs and, where desirable, restructuring that can improve overall government effectiveness within this subsector.

Training and human resource development within government is, in general, a good public investment. To improve governance, however, the training and sensitization must also include programs that are capable of addressing anti-corruption efforts. Tools to address these needs are available[7] and should be administered with a high priority to all involved in the natural resource sector. In addition, the following specific elements and messages must be incorporated within the specific sectors for which new agencies are emerging:

- ■ In fisheries, sensitization is required not just of those in the line agencies (MNRT, MALE, and eventually DSFA) but also in districts and partner organizations. Establishment of reporting networks involving enforcement authorities and citizens has

---

7. The World Bank anti-corruption resources are available publicly and are updated on a continuous basis. These are available at: http://web.worldbank.org.

been effective in Tanzania in the past (such as with controlling dynamite fishing) and remains a cost-effective means for complementing formal structures. One important message is that fines should not be regarded as a form of compensation for illegal activities, as such fines are seldom adequate to cover the administrative costs of enforcement or the damages caused by the illegal activities.

▨ Similarly in forestry and wildlife sectors, training and sensitization at the district level is paramount irrespective of the type of executive agencies that are ultimately put in place. Such training can and should commence ahead of any specific implementation of an EA.

Improved transparency and accounting systems must also be supported through all sectors. Some efforts are underway in all sectors and all require further strengthening. Some specific priorities within the individual sectors are as follows:

▨ In marine fisheries, support for establishing and maintaining the MCS database is of utmost importance and these need to meet an international standard (other systems in the country are less likely to come under international scrutiny). At present, the database is limited in scope and accessibility, with no integrated access nodes connecting government agencies or enforcement officials. With improved access and openness, the information systems will improve accountability. Information pertaining to licenses must also be maintained, but with added security precautions to avoid potential fraud and permit such licenses to be enforced at international standards.

▨ In artisanal mining, there is an urgent need to establish a GPS/GIS mineral cadastral system database that is adequately transparent to award, manage, administer, and enforce mineral rights. The database should be further organized to permit follow-up on benefit distribution, collection, and reinvestment.

CHAPTER 3

Management: Correcting Policy Distortions and Improving Efficiency

The Business Case for Improved Management

The second pillar—management—focuses on more traditional sectoral resource management, such as elimination of price distortions, capture of resource rents, and reduction of waste and externalities. Some of these management interventions also imply institutional changes to permit a more efficient, and more equitable, distribution of benefits. Specific interventions relate to clarification and entrenchment of property rights, adjustments to resource pricing instruments or levels, removal of distorting taxes and subsidies, and supportive institutional restructuring.

Improved management can have beneficial impacts in a number of ways. First, the property rights and resource management regime itself has an effect on the efficiency of resource use. In the absence of clear ownership or management responsibility, different interests will have a tendency to extract resources at rates that exceed optimal levels. Such "open access" conditions can give the appearance of higher short-term growth, but it in effect involves consumption of the capital or wealth asset. The rapid decrease in resource stocks can have other undesirable technical externalities, such as sedimentation of rivers (from deforestation), collapse of fishery stocks (from overfishing), or damage to aquifers (from overabstraction of groundwater). Social externalities are also often associated with open access conditions, as poorer sectors of the population may become further marginalized because of resource loss or because they do not have access to equipment or expertise that permits sustainable resource use. Strengthening of property rights regimes thus facilitates efficient resource management.

Second, resource pricing reforms may be in order if current systems lead to inefficiencies. Even where property rights are clear, the state is typically one of the interested participants as original owner of the resource. In turn for granting access or partial ownership, the state collects payments associated with resource development or extraction; such payments can be in the form of royalties, stumpage prices, lease payments, or similar arrangements. They are mechanisms for capturing the state share of domestic rents. The payments are typically distinguished from other taxation mechanisms (especially VAT, duties, or income taxes) that are levied at points other than resource production and are more usually in line with other tax measures in other industries (such as corporate income tax). Correct resource pricing is important for similar reasons as clarity in property rights. Provision of free resources (with no benefit flowing back to the state) may cause overextraction of the asset, while restrictive pricing regimes may discourage investment and cause under-use of the resource. This underutilization may appear to be protective in nature but it may also have the perverse effect that the resource manager loses interest in proper resource management because of its high cost of production; the resource is then not well maintained and may lose quality characteristics to its eventual value. The specific regime for resource pricing can also be important; net royalty systems are in theory more efficient than gross royalty systems, but they have higher information requirements and may thus not be appropriate in environments where production and accounting systems are not easily monitored. Similarly, auction methods for leases are an economically efficient means for extracting rents but may be less effective where there is no open competitive market. A proper resource pricing system is thus a function of both price levels as well as pricing regime; implementation of a proper system will lead to efficient resource extraction and retention of a fair share of the rent for the state.

Third, distortions arising from the taxation and subsidy system can also lead to inefficiencies for the economy as a whole. Distortions can arise if preferential treatment (either positive or negative) is applied to a given sector, where such distortions result in imbalances in local labor or capital markets. Examples of this typically involve specialized taxation treatment, or the provision of other inputs at artificially low market prices (this may correspond to improper pricing of other commodities, but not necessarily reflect pricing of the resource itself). Some of the single most significant subsidies in the tourism sector worldwide, for example, have involved the provision of free land, free water, or cheap power to entice hotel development as a part of economic development initiatives. Such subsidies often created over-investment that created social and environmental externalities. In Tanzania, for example, non-adherence to setback requirements on waterfront areas have been a *de facto* hidden land subsidy to the tourism sector that has contributed to foreshore erosion and placed some fragile coastal ecosystems at risk. The presence of such distortions is not always obvious but preferential treatment of industries or activities often points to potential distortions.

The fourth element of inefficient management we consider here is linked to unfair distribution of the costs or benefits associated with a given sector or activity. This is often foremost a social issue linked to participation in decisionmaking and equitable sharing of entitlements and responsibilities, but it quickly becomes an issue that can affect efficient management. The most common feedback occurs through the generation of conflicts in the face of real *or perceived* inequities; such conflicts themselves lead to inefficient management because they create incentives for overharvesting, place property rights in question, and increase administrative costs of compliance monitoring and enforcement.

Another element of inefficient management is associated with excessive bureaucracy. Such bureaucracy can in fact be related to any of the above more general issues. Some management systems require greater information requirements (such as net royalty systems) than others (such as competitive bidding for licenses). The existence of an extensive bureaucratic monitoring and reporting system should not be regarded as *a priori* necessary for efficient resource management. Indeed, the reverse may be true. Excessive bureaucracy may in fact discourage investments and promote side-stepping of regulations—contributing to lapses in governance that just impose higher enforcement costs.

Chapter 1 provided some initial indication of weaknesses across all sectors but in this chapter we elaborate more fully, for each sector, the greatest lapses relating to property right clarity, resource pricing, taxation distortions, and distributional equity issues. For each sector, we will focus on the more pressing management distortions (management issues relating to carbon resources, for example, are dominated by property right issues and we therefore de-emphasize the other issues). We then draw on some positive experiences from Tanzania to conclude with recommendations for appropriate management interventions.

The Need for Improved Management—Sectoral Overview

Fisheries (Freshwater)

Although freshwater fisheries are generally well administered and fish enters markets freely, open access to inland fisheries poses a serious threat to their long-term sustainability. The freshwater bodies of Tanzania harbor a variety of fish, including Nile perch, sardine, tilapia, and catfish. The bulk of the catch comes from Lake Victoria and Lake Tanganyika, together yielding 85 percent of inland production. Other important water bodies are Lake Rukwa, Lake Nyasa, the Mtera dam reservoir, and Nyumba ya Mungu. The annual catch of Tanzania freshwater fishery over the last ten years has increased from 294,782 tons in 1993 to more than 300,000 tons in 2003 with most of the increase coming from the Lake Victoria Nile Perch yield. The corresponding revenues have increased from TSh31 billion in 1993 to TSh141 billion in 2003.

The volume of freshwater catch has remained relatively stable during the past ten years. Catch per unit effort (CPUE), by contrast, has started to decline (Figure 3.1). The trend in declining CPUE is an indication that freshwater fish catches are generally declining despite high demand. Over-fishing practices through illegal methods of fishing such as beach seine and small size nets have depleted fish resources. Absence of quotas for freshwater fisheries (through tradable permits or through fixed allocations) has also encouraged over-fishing. Corrective measures can be instituted to ensure the sustainability of the fisheries, including strengthening and enforcing fisheries regulations to deal with illegal fishing in Lake Victoria, and instituting surveillance and monitoring of major fishing grounds.

Fisheries (Marine)

Inefficiencies associated with marine fisheries are largely related to property right clarity and resource pricing. In addition, however, there are strong feedback effects that relate to the economic dependency of coastal communities on this resource. Most of the various

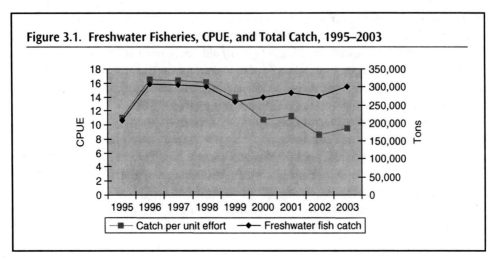

Figure 3.1. Freshwater Fisheries, CPUE, and Total Catch, 1995–2003

Source: Fisheries Department.

islands in the coastal area have no formal property rights, and many are not directly mapped against coastal districts. The areas have thus been regarded as open fishing grounds and disputes over fishery closures have been well documented (Walley 2004). Attempts to create protected areas or marine parks have often been stymied by the lack of clear property rights. More recently, success is being achieved through engagement of local community groups, but uncertainties associated with administrative jurisdictions persist in the territorial seas (to 12 nautical miles).

There is evidence that catches are decreasing across the range of reef and inshore species, and this is affecting artisanal fisheries that are operating at the limits of the traditional technologies. The destruction of habitats by dynamite fishing and poisoning causes concern for the future of these fisheries. Artisanal fisheries are socially and economically important activities for the coastal communities, but the systems put in place for monitoring the conservation of these areas appear inadequate. From the fragmentary data available, coastal and prawn fisheries are surpassing the Maximum Sustainable Yield (MSY).

Another major factor concerning EEZ fisheries (out to the 200 nautical mile limit) is that the stocks are generally migratory and their appearance in Tanzanian waters is seasonal. There is a distinct season from September to February only. This has made stock assessments problematic; there is no baseline study of stocks and no figures for Maximum Sustainable Yield (MSY) for the total pelagic fishery. However, some estimates exist for tuna and tuna-like species in the Western Indian Ocean from the Indian Ocean Tuna Commission (IOTC).

Yellow-fin tuna catches in the Indian Ocean were extraordinarily high during 2003 and 2004, while skipjack and big-eye remained at their average levels. Catches in 2003 represented a record year for all fleets that reported to the IOTC Secretariat. The catch includes younger, lower weight tuna for canneries, caught by seine vessels, and larger fish for the sashimi market caught by longliners. These anomalous catches occurred all over the western

Indian Ocean, and particularly in a small area in eastern Africa. The fish caught were of large sizes (100–150 cm). The management advice of the IOTC was that total catches of yellow-fin were close to or possibly above MSY. In these circumstances, any further increase in both effective fishing effort and catch above 2000 levels should be avoided. While the MSY estimated by IOTC is 280,000 to 350,000 tons per year, the 2003 annual catch was 400,000 to 450,000 tons and the average annual catch over the last five years was 326,000 tons (Chopin 2005).

In 2004, Private Fisheries Agreements (PFAs) were the basis for all longliner and tuna seiner fishing operations in the Tanzanian EEZ. The PFAs specify the financial compensation and license conditions associated with access to the resource. There are significant deficiencies in PFAs regarding responsible management of the fisheries. Specifically the PFAs for these fleets have not:

- Set limits on the catches that can be made by individual vessels or fleets;
- Generated the quantity and quality of fisheries information required to assess reliably the catch and effort of foreign fleets;
- Provided reliable estimates of the value of fish removals from the EEZ;
- Achieved a measurable level of compliance of the fishing fleets or deterred illegal, unreported or unobserved fishing activity;
- Enhanced the coastal state's understanding of the EEZ pelagic fisheries nor fostered the development of a Tanzanian capacity to contribute to management of these fisheries in a rational manner;
- Contributed to establishing an accurate EEZ catch history that could be used to justify future resource sharing formulas in the RFOs; and
- Provided the basis for a cooperative partnership between coastal and fishing states wherein the financial benefits are disbursed equitably between the relevant parties and the resource is exploited in a sustainable manner.

Resource rent estimates from marine fisheries captured by the PFAs show that license fees as a percentage of revenue generate a gross resource rent of approximately 2.2 percent. This is slightly less than half of what might be expected in a western industrial fishery. Calculations for tuna seiners vary somewhat more depending on different catch scenarios. Although the current license fee arrangements of PFAs in the EEZ generate substantial revenue, the level is too low to capture a reasonable resource rent (5 to 7 percent of gross revenue) for the coastal state. The PFAs as currently offered to foreign fishing enterprises are hence considered untenable.

Forestry

Administrative and governance weaknesses discussed previously contribute to unclear property rights and also to potential resource use conflict at the community level. In addition, economic value is being lost because of inefficient management systems associated with incorrect resource pricing that leads to open access conditions.

The NFP estimates that 95 percent of Tanzania's total wood consumption was attributed to wood fuel in 1999 (40.4 million m^3). Out of this, 26 million m^3 was consumed in the rural areas as fuelwood and 13.4 million m^3 in urban areas, mainly as charcoal. Open access and incorrect resource pricing is most obvious in fuelwood and charcoal production. A large number of rural industries rely on the use of wood fuel in their production processes. These are—in order of priority—tobacco curing, fish smoking, salt production, brick making, bread baking, tea drying, pottery, lime production, and beeswax processing. Additional large sinks for fuelwood in rural areas are beer brewing and alcohol distillation. Mostly, these are non-farm activities and one needs to keep in mind their environmental costs when promoting non-farm activities in rural areas as a means of economic growth.

Surprisingly, the NFP predicts that annual wood fuel consumption is not expected to increase, but to remain at the 1999 level of 40 million m^3. At the historical royalty rate of TSh3000 per m^3 this amounts to over 100 billion shillings per year that is not captured; the low resource prices result in overconsumption of wood in the face of uncertain property right regimes.

Other non-timber products suffer similarly from underpricing and loss of tax base. The price offered by the world market for gum coming from Tanzania is low compared to other countries. This is partly because of poor quality control and lack of gum grading arising from the mixing of gums from different sources. There is no local industry consuming gum, hence 99 percent of the collected gum is exported. The methods used for transfer pricing permit gum exporters to pay little or no income taxes in Tanzania.

Wildlife

Efficient wildlife management remains stymied by a number of factors, including unclear property rights and the collection of fees associated with wildlife use and resource pricing. This has also resulted in uncertainties and conflicts over benefit sharing, with many perceiving that current arrangements are unfair. Also, the quota system itself is ineffective and may not reflect ecological constraints. Hunting outside of quota and a general lack of respect for the law by the members of the private sector has prompted the Director of Wildlife to issue a Call for Compliance to all hunting outfitters in 2004. However, no serious effort to prosecute violations has been observed.

Wildlife Management Areas (WMAs) are described in the 1998 Wildlife Policy as land areas managed by communities to provide substantial tangible benefits from wildlife conservation. The regulations detailing WMA procedures were released with a four-year delay at the end of 2002. These regulations list 16 pilot areas in Tanzania where the concept of WMAs is being tested over a three-year period ending in 2005. A number of applications for establishment of WMAs within these pilot areas have been submitted to the Wildlife Division, but no permanent (non-pilot) WMA has so far been formally established.

Consequently, the full roll-out and development of WMAs is seriously delayed. There is little progress on development of an effective schedule for sharing of benefits from tourist hunting with the local communities on whose land hunting takes place. There is a general hesitation among outfitters to accept the WMA concept. It is possible that much of the delay in the development of WMAs is the result of a negative high-level influence by some hunting operators, who reportedly have influence with the government to block the allocation process. This may also arise from the interference that lingers from multiple administrative authorities (which may be resolved if an Executive Agency is established).

Another criticism is that the above regulations fail to place any real control of the WMAs in the hands of the communities as was originally envisaged. It is widely known that hunting will be the major source of income from WMAs, but scrutiny of the regulations reveals that the WD will regain full control over the appointment of outfitters to operate the WMAs and what they are allowed to hunt by controlling the quotas. Part of the issue is that ownership of animals is retained by the state; government interprets this as a basis for maintaining control centrally instead of delegating certain management functions. This means of regulation is inefficient.

Further constraints to community involvement in wildlife related business is that commercial success in mainstream hunting and tourism business requires large upfront investment, commercial experience and substantial risk-taking behavior. These often present barriers of entry for local entrepreneurs or community level organizations. Rural credit is scarce, familiarity with the international tourism sector is limited, and hospitality skills are low. Community partnerships might be a way of tackling some of these constraints. Another means is to attract foreign partners but current license allocation procedures deliberately favor Tanzanians, making it difficult to attract such partnerships.

Concessions are leased at rates below true market value and represent a loss of income to the Wildlife Division estimated at over US$7 million. Many concessions are leased to outfitters without the capacity to market or manage their own hunting operations. The system thus promotes subleasing to foreigners with a result that much of the income generated by the industry never enters the country and the Tanzania Revenue Authority does not access much of the funds that should be due for taxation.

Tourism

While the market for tourism in Tanzania is well developed, the major shortfall in tourism is that it focuses on a narrow range of products for collecting government rents associated with the resource. Figure 3.2 illustrates that the fee base is particularly lop-sided, with little being extracted through concession arrangements (which tend to be a major revenue source in other countries). In effect, this is equivalent to an under-pricing of the resource. For example, an economic study conducted in 2002–03 revealed that TANAPA receives less income from high-end tours using hotels and lodges than from budget tours staying in campsites. For TANAPA to benefit from high-end tourism as opposed to mass tourism, they need to capture more high-end revenue by re-evaluating lodging concessions fees or encouraging and developing more specialty camping. TANAPA's park entrance fees are comparable to those of Kenya with the fee to the most popular parks averaging US$25. Tanzania charges the highest fees for vehicles, compared to Kenya, Botswana and South Africa.

From this, it appears as if TANAPA could exploit its potential for revenue generation more fully. Compared to other parks in competing destinations, TANAPA parks have more activities run by external tour operators, leaving substantial revenue in the hands of foreign investors, while only charging 2 percent for concessions. Other parks, for example in Botswana, offer additional activities not available in Tanzania, such as lake boating, fishing, overnight trips, or bush breakfast.

A second management inefficiency is the contribution that tourism can make within the overall socio-economic development context and to poverty alleviation. The potential for improving the local development impact is still not fully exploited. In the Mara-Serengeti ecosystem, the number of households earning any income from tourism varies from

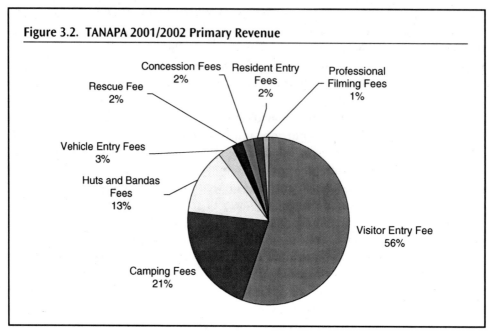

Figure 3.2. TANAPA 2001/2002 Primary Revenue

Source: TANAPA, "Maximizing Revenues in Tanzania National Parks: Towards a better understanding of park choice and nature tourism in Tanzania," (undated).

86 percent in Talek (Kenya) to about 10 percent in the Ngorongoro Conservation Area. Overall, tourism is not prominent in the Tanzanian 2001 Rural Development Strategy, which acknowledges the need for growth in rural areas through non-farm economic growth but without specifying the role and potential of tourism. Still, there are examples of how tourism can be of substantial (financial) benefit to local communities. In Loliondo Division in Ngorongoro District, seven villages earn a total of over US$110,000 annually from joint ventures with wildlife tour operators. In Ololosokwan village, tourism revenue totals about US$55,000 annually. This income has large poverty reduction potential in a dryland area that does not offer many economic diversification possibilities.

Mining

Most analyses show that Tanzanian mining taxation is consistent with international trends, in the interests of investment competitiveness. To attract capital, tax incentives have historically been generous towards foreign interests. Individually negotiated development agreements have provided generous tax relief that may include, for example, no duty on capital goods, and 100 percent initial capital allowance. Royalties are generally low: gold mining attracts a gross royalty of 3 percent, diamonds attract 5 percent, rough and unpolished gemstones attract 5 percent, while polished gemstones are royalty-free. The main recommendations for reform in this area call for a standard treatment of mining taxation (eliminate individually negotiated development agreements); the application of a standard rate of depreciation for all new investments; and the removal of special tax relief in favor of VAT deferment.

Overall weak monitoring has also resulted in open access in those areas that are not correctly licensed and documented. Lack of coordination between government departments has led to incorrect mineral production and sales records while the bureaucratic burden of registration and reporting has increased informal mining and marketing operations. Small-scale operations are restricted to Tanzanian citizens, companies or cooperatives that can hold a claim for one year, after which it must be renewed yearly. Claim holders must pay royalties, submit returns, and pay annual licensing fees. Claims are cancelled for non-compliance with reporting procedures. The procedural burden alone has resulted in evasion, which in turn has increased compliance monitoring costs and introduced inefficiencies in the sector.

An additional issue is that of perceived favoritism, which leads to conflict in some areas. A common perception is that foreign mining companies pay little tax on huge revenues. Part of the problem stems from a general lack of understanding of the tax regime, which is complicated by the existence of individually negotiated development agreements with large-scale operators. The perception is also fostered by the lack of income retention in local mining areas. The central government does not hypothecate mining revenue to subnational levels, and public finance at the subnational level is weak. Consequently, local mining community authorities lack the necessary funds to deal with the social and environmental impacts of mining. The environmental impacts of both large- and small-scale has been a cause for public concern.

Carbon Resources

As noted previously, the development and trade of emission reductions remains in its infancy, and is to some degree hampered by inadequate institutional arrangements and the lack of responsible agencies. At a management level, one test case has shown the inadequacies of management instruments within this young sector. The TIST program is a small-holder tree growing initiative that has been in place in East Africa (Kenya, Uganda, Tanzania) since 1999. It permits small community groups (typically 10 members) to use small areas of land to grow trees (at least 1000 trees per group). Verification of tree growth and conditions is done through locally trained individuals with interests or backgrounds in silviculture, using state-of-the-art GPS-based systems that permit accurate tracking of tree inventories. Through these mechanisms, TIST has managed to carry and monitor an inventory of about 150,000 trees in Tanzania (in two project areas near Dodoma and Morogoro) and assign emission reduction credits to the smallholders. The volume of ERs for the program as a whole is adequate to permit TIST to engage in formal open market transactions with international buyers and donor agencies; transactions can also be entered into by private individuals since mid-2006 on the voluntary market on eBay. Payments to the tree owners are small, of the order of TSh20 per tree annually, but are done in a timely manner and provide cash income while also supporting locally important tree crops. Payments are made directly to established community organizations with written management plans and revenue sharing agreements. Overall, this model has demonstrated that carbon trade can benefit local initiatives and that modern technology can be applied to monitor conditions under acceptable international standards. The management issue, however, with these projects is the assignation of property rights. Most countries in the region have legal and regulatory mechanisms in place that may assign use rights or access rights to forest or timber resources, but the property right regime over carbon is typically not defined. The same applies to Tanzania.

This lack of a firm definition of property rights has direct impacts on payments in the form of the traded price of the ERs; with unclear rights there are fewer buyers willing to take on the risk of purchasing these ERs and converting them to certified ERs that command a high price. Since the initiation of trading under the CDM, world prices for ERs have at times exceeded US\$20 per ton of CO_2 but prices offered to developing countries with poor property right regimes have typically been in the US\$7 per ton case. For forestry projects with smallholders, which involve other uncertainties and risks, negotiated prices are of the order of US\$3 to US\$4 per ton of CO_2. Improvements in the property right regime through clarifying ownership will thus directly result in higher prices to stakeholders, improved export earnings, and enhanced opportunities for revenue sharing at the local level.

Improved Management Examples in Tanzania

The above discussion illustrates that the sector remains plagued by inefficient management regimes. Some of these are linked to poor governance (discussed in the previous chapter) but others are a reflection of management weakness, or in the structure of management arrangements. In principle, many of these poor management arrangements are easier to correct than issues associated with poor governance. Models of success are available from within the sector itself, and replication of these—or building upon them—would generate positive results.

Property Right Reforms

Tanzania does contain within its legislation and policies significant attempts to clarify property rights through entrenching some management tasks with local communities. This is especially the case where communities are close to or within the natural resource areas. Wildlife management, forestry management and marine park management are all being undertaken to various degrees with increased community management. This activity can generate substantial revenues to local community or district coffers.

A case in point is that associated with honey production. The new Forest Policy and the National Beekeeping Programme oversees the establishment of village beekeeping reserves. In 2003 villages in five districts have established such reserves, from which they will accrue direct cash income. The average annual export of apiculture products between 1993 and 2003 was 348.8 tons of honey and 187 tons of beeswax, which generated average export earnings of US\$1 158 000 for honey and US\$211 000 for beeswax.

Resource Pricing Reforms

Government is generally aware that under-pricing of resources leads to both their mis-management (through excess exploitation) and to a loss in current revenue for government coffers. Some reforms have been undertaken to correct this. In large scale mining for example, royalty rates and their associated fiscal regimes reflect competitive pricing and best practice in many respects. Also, in spite of administrative issues associated with forestry management, royalty take has been increasing in that sector. Royalties from timber sales are the most important source of income for the sector; they represent 85 percent of income, amounting to almost TSh5 billion in recent years. Registration fees for dealers of forest products were the second largest source of revenue. Revenue from registration fees has been increasing steadily over the last three years.

Tax/Subsidy Reforms

Removal of subsidies has occurred in Tanzania in a number of areas that traditionally provided free goods or services. The Tanzania government's 2002 National Water Policy, for example, promotes decentralization of authority to river basins and provides mechanisms for local authorities to secure property rights and impose user charges on water. In other areas, land use planning is also being better managed with decentralized authority. This land use planning seeks to establish clearer land tenure policies and avoid the give-away of land without proper compensation. The result is also positive for decreasing or entirely eliminating adverse environmental impacts; enforcement of setback regulations, for example, protects coastal margins from improper construction techniques.

Supportive Institutional Restructuring

Perhaps the greatest institutional support that can be given to efficient management of the sector is not within government itself, but to providing an investment environment that is conducive to responsible investment by the private sector. Numerous examples are already evident within Tanzania in the forestry, park management, and mining areas. Partnerships with the private sector in plantation management have improved revenues and decreased operational and compliance monitoring costs. In park management in Zanzibar, for example, Chumbe Island Marine Park is entirely operated and managed by a private sector party that has a lease on the park, provides tourism facilities, promotes conservation education in the local community, and enforces park regulations. In mining, large-scale mining companies are working with the legal small-scale miners by, for example, providing them with improved technology in exchange for their production. The aim is to reduce illegal activity while increasing the efficiency of the ASMs. Large-scale operators have adopted a participatory policy for new projects.

Recommended Priority Management Actions

Improvements in management efficiency can often be realized more quickly than those associated with extensive institutional reforms. Because much of the legislation and policy work is already in place to permit more efficient regulatory mechanisms, management improvements may involve just changes to implementing regulations. This is certainly the case for the two sectors with the most extensive management inefficiency: marine fisheries and wildlife. Some of the interventions below thus represent continuations of on-going exercises. A sector-by-sector list of key interventions is provided in the Appendix; the following summarizes the key recommendations.

Property right issues still persist in most sectors, creating open access conditions and their associated inefficiencies. Strengthening is warranted in all areas, and this includes especially the area of community property rights over resources such as forestry and wildlife. Recommended interventions in other specific areas include the following:

- *The establishment of a community territorial sea* will greatly improve the management efficiency around nearshore coastal waters in the marine fisheries sector. Such community territorial seas typically extend out to less than the national territorial seas (which goes out to 12 nm) and they do not conflict with this national territorial sea. Other countries (Philippines, Indonesia) use this concept with success, and it essentially involves recognizing, documenting and supporting management rights and responsibilities of the coastal districts over this area of water. Administrative boundaries between districts can be extended into the sea, and community rights can also be defined associated with individual coastal villages. The concept is being pursued under one of the activities of the MACEMP project for testing in some pilot areas, but will require national support for roll-out to more than the MACEMP pilot districts. Devolution of some responsibility to the community level (especially in monitoring) will complement national efforts and reduce the implementation costs of patrols and enforcement.
- *Work on a cadastral system* for supporting the licensing and regularization of artisanal mining is both an urgent governance and management issue. The system must be satisfactorily independent and transparent to award, manage, administer and enforce mineral rights.
- *Establish a legal framework for community and other rights over carbon resources.* This grey area requires immediate attention in the form of legislative reviews and drafts to permit proper definition of community rights over emission reductions.

Resource pricing interventions include primarily the reform of licensing systems and structures. The most pressing are those in marine fisheries and wildlife.

- *Reform and harmonization of the licensing system in the offshore fisheries* area is necessary to increase rent collection and move to encourage improved compliance. In the absence of reliable stock information, the use of bidding systems may be the optimal solution in the long term. In the near-term, standard licensing structures and fees may be appropriate, although at higher levels than those that have been historically applied.
- *Changes in the wildlife license scheme* must be instituted to create a more open market and permit a higher rent share to accrue to government. An open bidding auction lease system is proposed, using transparent structures that require bidders to pre-qualify and show technical and financial competence. If some auctions will include some form of domestic preference arrangements, the nature of those arrangements (in terms of bidding penalty percentage on foreign bidders) must be clearly specified. Joint venture bids with domestic leads should be treated as domestic bidders in such auctions.

The greatest distortions arising from *subsidies and tax* structures also lie in the area of marine fisheries and wildlife. Raw export of the resource and avoidance of taxation is as much the fault of the fiscal regime as it is of the overall regulatory environment. For example, incentives enjoyed by other sectors for value-added processing are not being accessed effectively by entrepreneurs. At this stage, there has been no specific review of taxation impacts within these sectors, although there are indications that the tax system could be used effectively to encourage development within these sectors and also to provide incentives for regularizing currently illegal activities. This paper calls for a more extensive review of the potential use of fiscal instruments in these sectors. In addition, in the mining sector, the most important ongoing reform is the uniform application of a fiscal regime, with appropriate arrangements for collection, distribution and use of benefits.

Supportive *institutional interventions* are most necessary in the areas of fisheries, wildlife, tourism, and mining. In these sectors there still persists real or perceived distributional issues that threaten overall management efficiency. Increased reliance on private sector partnerships, and co-management regimes is warranted.

CHAPTER 4

Precaution: Introducing Safety Nets and Accommodating Uncertainty

The Role of Precaution and Redundancy

A third area of concern—protection of the resource asset—is less familiar to many planners, but critical within the context of economic planning in a complex yet vulnerable natural resource sector. The reality is that the sector has become less resilient to external shocks, and such shocks (fishery collapses, droughts, tsunamis, extinction, avian flu) are becoming part of the experience and living memory of the current generation of Tanzanians. Such shocks also exacerbate social inequalities, which in turn can lead to increased conflict over scarce resources; the conflict invariably leads to resource management inefficiencies and concomitant economic losses. In the same way that Tanzania is putting into place social safety nets for its labor force (NSSF), there are also appropriate safety net mechanisms and strategies available for protecting the natural resource sector. Many interventions associated with protection may be equally considered as means for improving institutional effectiveness or general resource management. In this chapter, we review some lessons about precautionary planning, explore some options, and then place these within Tanzania's context.

Some Stylized Lessons: Why Precautionary Policies are Different

There has been growing experience with precautionary approaches internationally, which can also be regarded more generally as "no regret" strategies, in that they reduce the possibility of worst possible outcomes. Over the very long term, many would argue that these precautionary policies are also economically efficient, and that they could thus be included within a standard set of reforms that permit management efficiency. However, there are some lessons about precautionary policies that seem counter-intuitive to some and even appear to contradict standard prescriptions for resource management. This is because such standard prescriptions are often done in the context of a single sector with all other things assumed constant ("ceteris paribus"); precautionary approaches try to capture broader effects in other sectors, in conditions of uncertainty, in circumstances of system instability, and other features more common in complex systems. Some of the attributes of precautionary policies can be characterized as follows:

- ▨ *Redundancy is a positive attribute.* Redundancy, or duplication of function, is a valid strategy within a complex system. This may impose short-term costs, but it ensures greater continuity of critical components of the overall system. In conventional planning, specialization of function and elimination of duplication is often regarded as desirable in the spirit of cost-effectiveness but this mode of planning can undermine long-term stability. An example of desirable duplication is that of staff training in circumstances of high AIDS/HIV incidence; we may know that the organization is vulnerable to loss of life but—because we do not know who will die— it is justifiable to provide training in core functions to a higher complement of staff than might usually be trained.
- ▨ *Stress is not necessarily bad.* Stress in a system builds resilience because those subject to facing new manageable challenges on an ongoing basis will develop the skills and confidence to handle major unforeseen shocks. The role of safety nets and precautionary measures therefore is not to eliminate stress or provide everyone with an easy life. Indeed, precautionary programs can in fact provide training in stress management and adaptation through simulation of stressful circumstances under controlled situations.
- ▨ *Decisionmaking is best carried out by those most directly affected by resource degradation.* This precept often goes against the entrenched norms in centralized systems that are built on models of high level oversight and management. These centralized systems are also often further encumbered by prejudices that those affected (often the poor or uneducated) are not qualified to make decisions or manage the situations. Practical experience consistently demonstrates that those close to the resource base are qualified to make decisions, and can often react in a more timely fashion and more appropriately to early warning signs. This is not to say that there is no role for centralized authorities (in monitoring or coordinating, for example) but the roles are shared in a clearly defined structure that respects each party's relative strengths.
- ▨ *Safety nets can be seen as entitlements.* At a psychological level, individuals are more attached to property or uses that they have historically enjoyed, than to that same property or use if offered to them as a future opportunity.[8] This attachment to perceived entitlements also, however, provides a strong basis for safety net interventions. Precautionary approaches that protect entitlements, or reinforce these attachments, are generally more effective than those that try to create new entitlements. Practically speaking, protecting access to traditional uses of fisheries, forests, or wildlife

---

8. Empirically this is manifested as higher willingness to accept compensation (WTAC) for the loss of a unit of good than willingness to pay (WTP) for the provision an extra unit of the same good. In experiments and real situations, the WTAC is often an order of magnitude—up to ten times—higher than the WTP.

is more meaningful than an equivalent monetary compensation in new income earning opportunities. This is an important lesson because, again, it is contrary to received traditional planning models where the two are regarded as roughly equivalent. Certainly they may be equivalent from a public expenditure perspective (in terms of income foregone from the resource versus income provided through an alternative livelihood) but as a safety net the protection of entitlements is in fact more cost-effective.

■ *Uncertainty and surprises are the norm.* Small scale planning can often proceed under conditions of relative certainty, with fluctuations in parameters well established through historical monitoring programs. In larger complex systems, however, greater levels of uncertainty persist, and surprises are more common. Surprises are those situations for which there is no historical context or precedent. The incidence of such surprises is expected to increase because of global factors such as climate change, which is providing new challenges (as well as opportunities) in many countries. Fertile areas may become more drought prone, watershed management efforts may be undermined by forest cover loss, coastal areas may become more threatened by increased storm surge, and new diseases threatening humans, plants and animals may find toe-holds in areas that have been heretofore untouched. Some planning tools that form the basis of carefully designed management efforts—such as calculations of "carrying capacity" or "sustainable yield"—become singularly meaningless in the face of such surprises.

Available Approaches and Options

Interventions that perform a safety net function include a wide variety of instruments, including some that are intended specifically to address equity issues and social vulnerability. In general the ones that interest us are those that decrease vulnerability or, conversely, increase the resilience of the system. The system's resilience is a concept borrowed from ecology, and in effect involves any intervention that is capable of improving an entity's ability to adapt to changing circumstances. The safety net options we focus on here as practical options include the following:

■ *Implementation of revenue retention schemes.* The standard economic model of tax efficiency is that funds should not be ear-marked, but should flow to central coffers for subsequent redistribution. This model applies well where there is strong administrative efficiency, effective reallocation, and high levels of transparency. These conditions rarely exist, even in industrialized countries. Under a wide range of circumstances, therefore, some form of ear-marking of collected revenues is both administratively efficient and socially desirable. Retention systems that keep revenues closer to their source of earning, fall into this category; where clear redistribution mechanisms exist that involve local affected communities or individuals they also provide a potential safety net mechanism for guarantying basic services or incomes. They can also respond more rapidly to sudden changes in circumstances.

■ *Promotion of explicit adaptive co-management models that involve local, national and regional participants.* The concept of adaptive co-management (ACM) has received increased currency and is being implemented in more field situations. The basic tenets of ACM are that it promotes adaptation through involving multiple stakeholders in a learning environment that is dedicated to long-term sustainability (Plummer and Armitage 2006). Responsibilities and entitlements are well defined, but may themselves be flexible. Minority positions are respected and full participation is encouraged. Its success as a safety net mechanism occurs at many levels. Decisionmaking is locally based, but supported by higher national or regional authorities. Experimentation and learning is encouraged, which builds resilience through trial and error processes followed by replication. Respect for minority positions minimizes conflict in the long-term. Duplication and redundancy is often implicit because different stakeholders will need to be able to share in each other's roles at times. Also, ACM implicitly includes distributional elements that can provide income relief when necessary.

- *Investments in education and awareness building*, complemented by understandable norms and standards. Investments in education, across as broad a base as possible, improve system resilience both through teaching adaptive skills and creating redundancy. When complemented by well-published norms (for water quality or health standards, for example) they tend to be self-reinforcing in the long term.

- *Enhanced vulnerability monitoring.* The key to this activity is providing a long-term monitoring profile that permits stakeholders to detect and respond to abnormal variations. Contrary to received procedures in many planning models, baseline conditions are not necessarily relevant in such circumstances. What is relevant is that monitoring continues on a regular basis, and that the information is provided on a timely basis to those with a stake or interest.

- *Investments that increase or protect diversification opportunities.* These can fall into a number of categories. The first type is that associated with new opportunities that are not linked to existing activities, and is the traditional economic development approach to diversification. Development of new industries or new technologies falls into this category, and it is often seen as a compensation mechanism. It is often constrained by willingness or ability of local populations (especially the poor) to engage in such new opportunities. A second type is increasing activity of associated activities; introducing new ways to do the same types of things. Examples include value-added processing in NTFPs or new gear types in fishing. These may not address, however, the underlying vulnerability (from fishery collapse or forest degradation). A third type, which we regard as the most sustainable, involves protection of the resource base and permitting local communities to manage historical entitlements or uses. This latter type of investment creates positive feedback effects that reinforce sustainable management.[9]

---

9. Based on Noack and Ruitenbeek (Forthcoming 2007). These three alternative diversification strategies are referred to as decoupling, weak coupling, and strong coupling depending on their reliance on the resource base. Strong coupling strategies (based on analyses of community conservation efforts and models in East Africa) have been found to be the most sustainable in the long-term.)

The Need for Precaution: Sectoral Overview

Fisheries

As noted previously, fisheries provides a basic livelihood and subsistence source of protein for millions of Tanzanians, both in freshwater areas as well as on the coastal margins. The vulnerability of these communities has been demonstrated both from internally generated shocks as well as unexpected external influences. Local fishers have been affected negatively by illegal near-shore industrial fishing that, in a matter of days, can wipe out entire coral reef habitats from illegal use of trawling nets. Perhaps the most dramatic example is that associated with the EU fishery ban in 1999 that resulted subsequently in a complete reorganization of the Lake Victoria fishery and processing industry.

A major fish industry had developed around Lake Victoria, shared by Tanzania (51 percent), Uganda (43 percent), and Kenya (6 percent), with annual revenues from fish exports amounting to over US$200 million. Over half a million people were earning their living from the fishing and processing of Nile perch from the lake and local supplier companies were also deriving considerable benefits from the fish industry. In 1999, after suspected fish poisoning, an EU export ban was imposed on Lake Victoria fish. The three countries, in particular Tanzania and Uganda, suffered a tremendous loss. Fish exports from Uganda alone dropped dramatically by 50 percent in value between 1996 and 2000 and exports from Tanzania fell by almost the same level in 1999. In addition to the lost export earnings, one-third of the some 200,000 persons employed in the fishing industry lost their jobs. Many others saw their earnings fall to less than one-third of their normal income. Several fish factories either closed or were operating at as little as 20 percent capacity.

An integrated remedial approach and strategy laid the ground for a reliable fish safety assurance system. Steps were taken in parallel to improve the organizational and regulatory framework for the industry and to strengthen the capacities of fish inspection services, technical support institutions and in the private sector, at all stages of the industry from fishing to factory. Particular emphasis was placed on the establishment of working tools, guidelines, and methodologies (fish inspection manual, code of practice, inspection guides and records, and so forth).

Major upgrading of fish safety and quality assurance systems occurred at all levels of the production chain. The role of central regulatory authorities was streamlined and strengthened, and a fish inspection system was implemented in accordance with international requirements. Technical support institutions were supported with newly formulated working guidelines and tools. National experts have been trained in Good Hygiene Practices. Hazard Analysis and Critical Control Points have been implemented as a monitoring program on boats, at landing sites and in processing plants to ensure safety of exported fish products. The EU ban was lifted on all countries by the end of 2000, and Lake Victoria fish has regained its EU market share and is expanding to new markets (such as the United States).

In spite of this reorganization, however, the fishery remains vulnerable to shocks. Although the interventions improved both governance and management of the industry, they cannot be regarded as a safety net mechanism for the Tanzania fisheries. Illegal fishing still occurs and small users are being marginalized, particularly as lake levels fall from ongoing drought conditions and inadequate recharge in key watersheds.

Table 4.1. Sources of Income in Villages, Tanzania, 2002

Sources	Lushoto District	Kilimanjaro District	Meru District	Sample Averages
Crop production	157 704	138 010	360 000	218 571
Livestock	38 038	417 061	590 000	348 366
Off-farm	296 304	718 233	420 000	478 179
Environmental income	72 186	71 266	123 261	88 904
–NTFP	45 036	21 427	62 708	43 057
–Timber	1 200	2 100	504	1 268
–Poles	106	13 581	4 374	6 020
–Fuelwood	21 168	33 345	49 600	34 704
–Whithies	4 676	813	6 075	3 855
Sum	564 232	1 344 570	1 493 261	1 134 021

Source: Field data (2002); Ngaga, Chamshama, and Monela (2003).

Forestry

In the forestry sector, it is well known that dependency on the forest for charcoal or fuel wood affects millions. Loss of this product would strike the well being of numerous Tanzanians, and most notably those living in rural areas. But the potential vulnerability is greater still when one considers, also, other non-timber forest products (NTFPs) that contribute to this well being. Loss of forest thus reduces not just charcoal availability, but also key components of livelihood—components that would fall into what we above called an "entitlement" from the perspective of the users. The contribution of forests to food security is also indirect via soil quality services provided as an input to agricultural production. A direct contribution to food security is through NTFPs that have nutritional value such as mushrooms or gum (used by pastoralists and hunter gatherers). Table 4.1 illustrates that, among the environmental income sources, NTFPs contribute the largest share followed by fuel wood.

In one study, for example, charcoal, fuel wood, and wild fruits contribute 58 percent of the cash incomes of farmers in six villages surveyed (Monela and others 2000). Honey alone accounted for one third of all cash income in these villages. According to the surveyed farmers, agriculture had become less profitable, thus inducing them to find other means to earn a living, for example, collecting and selling forest produce. Infrastructure improvements have made it easier for them to bring their forest products to the markets of sale. Similarly, 94 percent of households surveyed in a study conducted in Shinyanga utilize wild vegetables as relish (Kagya 2002). Theostina (2003) demonstrates that 51 percent of residents in Morogoro use money accrued from sales of NTFPs to purchase food in times of food shortage. Forests hence also have a safety net function to poor people.

Biodiversity and Wildlife

Tanzania is among the four countries in the world classified as "megadiversity" nations,[10] because of the variety of habitats found in the country. The biological diversity has been

10. Other countries are Republic of Congo, Brazil, and Indonesia.

described in a number of studies and academic papers, including the Tanzania Country Study on Biological Diversity (1998). According to conservationists, Tanzania's biodiversity is under severe threat. For example, the country's coastal forests are remnants of some of the world's oldest forests. Burgess et al (1992) describe the biodiversity potential hosted by these forests. Collectively they support many rare and poorly known plant species, including around 50 believed to be endemic to a single forest, seven bird species and sub-species of global conservation significance. They also contain several rare mammals, reptiles and amphibians, and an invertebrate fauna with many rare species.

Tourism

The tourism sector has, over the past decades, been vulnerable to shocks that are at times completely unconnected to situations in Tanzania. Many of these are linked to regional, or even global, security concerns. While the U.S. embassy bombings in Tanzania and Kenya in 1998 provide obvious links to local circumstances, tourism continent-wide suffered markedly in response to other incidents that were not related to Tanzania. The deadly attacks on tourists at Luxor Egypt in 1997 impacted tourism throughout Africa. The Bwindi incident in Uganda in February 1999 in which eight tourists were killed had similar negative effects on regional tourism. General collapse of global travel and security in the wake of the September 11th attacks on the United States in 2001 also had repercussions throughout the tourism industry. All of these cases serve to show the vulnerability of the sector to external events.

Mining

The social and environmental vulnerabilities associated with the mining industry are widespread. Health services in mining communities are severely lacking given the particular problems in these areas. The dominant causes of morbidity and mortality are inadequate sanitary standards, mercury exposure, work-related accidents, tuberculosis, and sexually transmitted diseases including HIV/AIDS. The spread of HIV/AIDS in mining communities is high due to lack of awareness, transient labor, widespread prostitution, and lack of access to quality health services. Infection rate data are scarce, but surveys show that a relatively high percentage of people living in mining communities perceive HIV/AIDS to be a common disease, while the Mererani mining area is known to have one of the country's highest HIV prevalence rates.

Child labor is a particular concern in mining, often reflecting a high level of poverty in the mining areas. In the Geita District 12.5 percent of the workforce are children, with a greater prevalence in the small-scale operations than in the large-scale mines. The Mererani tanzanite mines have about 3,000 so-called "snake boys" who work in deep narrow mines. Child work participation is higher in gemstone areas than in gold-mining areas.

Women comprise about 25 percent of the ASM workforce, engaged directly or indirectly in mining activities. They face obstacles due to illiteracy, lack of access to credit, cultural barriers, and time constraints. Their salary is typically a third that of their male colleagues, a lower proportion than in most other industries, and they are typically trapped at a subsistence level of mining.

The most serious environmental impact of small-scale mining is mercury pollution of air and water bodies, with its negative impacts on human and animal life. It is estimated that in the mining area surrounding Lake Victoria, 1.2 tons of mercury are released to the environment for every 1 ton of artisanal gold. Large-scale mining also causes air and water pollution, as well as noise pollution and land degradation including deforestation. Various incidents have been reported, but there is no consensus as to the gravity and prevalence of the environmental damage from large-scale operations. Still, the scientific evidence notwithstanding, there is no doubt that mining activities are at least perceived as having serious negative impacts on the environment.

Long-term vulnerability is also related to the nature of the resource base itself, which is non-renewable. There is concern that exploration is inadequate to provide new mineral reserves for the future of the sector. For example, it is believed that 40 percent of the country's easy-to-find gold reserves have been found. Except for two, the remaining life of current operating mines is modest, which is an indication of the need to induce exploration and to identify new target areas. Such activity is medium- to long-term and could, if neglected, precipitate stagnation in the mineral sector and prompt investors to move to other countries with proven reserves. This vulnerability in the mining sector is further exacerbated by international market conditions. Mining communities are faced with the constant threat of mine closure. International prices fluctuations translate into more or less employment. To prepare for the impacts of a potential fall in mining activities, communities need to maintain or enhance the diversity of their economies.

Examples of Precautionary Management in Tanzania

Tanzania has some recent experience with precautionary instruments, although they were not necessarily designed with precautionary complex system principles in mind. Some examples of these follow.

Fisheries and the Marine Legacy Fund

The concept of the Marine Legacy Fund (MLF) is being developed under the World Bank MACEMP project with seed financing from the Global Environment Facility (GEF). It is expected to start pilot operations by 2009, with oversight by the DSFA. The concept is one of retention of revenues but from a diversity of sources; some share of revenues from marine parks, from fishery licenses, from coastal tourism, and from offshore oil, gas, and mineral development would all be retained by the MLF. In turn, the MLF will finance core operational expenses in key sectors, including fisheries, marine parks and tourism. Fund size is expected to be of the order of US$50 to US$100 million in due course, with average revenues over any five year period being capable of offsetting average core expenses. In effect, the MLF generates net outflows in deficit years when one sector may have been hit by some shock, while generating surpluses in other years. The fact that the different sectors (energy, tourism, fisheries) are subject to different types of shocks is a deliberate design to take advantage of the diversification and risk sharing.[11]

---

11. This is referred to as uncorrelated risks. By contrast, diversifying into different types of tourism is not necessarily an appropriate risk management strategy because all of the products are still subject to the same risks.

Safety Nets for the Mining Industry

There has been a steady growth of company-assisted improvements to social infrastructure including electricity generation, HIV/AIDS education programs, water supply, and sanitation. Improved technologies are being demonstrated and transferred to small-scale operators. Worker associations such as REMA and FEMETA are working to create dialogue with government on issues including stable mineral markets and training. The Chamber of Mines promotes environmental and human health protection, undertakes dispute resolution, and works with government on matters of wages, labor, and taxation.

The Diamond Development Initiative (DDI) pilot project in Tanzania recently (2006) received an injection of US$2 million from De Beers. The DDI represents a cross-section of industry, NGOs, and the donor community, that addresses problems of ASM, industry, and governments. Recognizing the problem of artisanal alluvial diamond mining, the goal of the initiative is to bring diamond ASMs into the formal sector. The Kimberley Process Certification Scheme, which was developed by the DDI, is a system to manage and certify internal and international trade in rough diamonds.

Revenue Retention in Forestry

The retention scheme allows the MNRT to retain 70 percent of the revenue collected from Forestry. The remaining 30 percent is submitted to the Treasury. After deductions of 14 percent of the retained revenue for the Ministry's central administration and other divisions, the remaining 56 percent of the originally collected revenue is allocated to FBD. With this income, the FBD finances all its recurrent (except for staff salaries that are paid by Treasury) and some development expenditures, though donor financing covers most activities. Local governments are allowed to retain for their own purposes 5 percent of the sum above TSh1 million of collected revenue.

Examples from Tanzania's Water Resources Assistance Strategy

Tanzania has recently adopted a comprehensive water resource assistance strategy (TWRAS) that will be funded with domestic resources and international donor support. The strategy provides an example of a comprehensive sector-specific precautionary approach that is designed to provide safety nets in vulnerable areas. The nature of the water sector is that, as noted previously, water can be a unifying theme in overall resource management.

The TWRAS contains a number of provisions that protect other resource values. These are organized around the following priority areas:

- *Water resource reforms at the local and basin levels.* Under this priority, the TWRAS supports new river and lake basin organizations in licensing, enforcement, and water quality and flow monitoring. Also, water user rights are strengthened, with particular emphasis on the marginalized and poor populations. In a regional context, transboundary water security issues around the three Great Lakes will be enhanced, as well as specific multipurpose developments at the Kagera River basin, the Regional Rusomo Falls Hydroelectric project, and the Mara River basin developments.

■ *Cross-sectoral coordination.* This priority involves a number of coordinating, aware-ness raising, and education functions that are also supported by protective mea-sures and clear standards and norms. Water allocations will be distributed within this context, and water quality standards will be further developed in support of providing better coordination. Water resources will be protected through control-ling pollution, and increasing awareness and support within the forestry and agri-cultural sectors where deforestation, soil erosion, and nutrient loss all contribute further to diminished water quality.

■ *Investments in protective infrastructure.* Such investments will remain an important component of the overall strategy, and go beyond standard technical interventions such as irrigation and WSS. In addition, investments will include support for the formation of water user groups, licensing of water extractions and discharge per-mits, and monitoring of water use. Private sector involvement is being encouraged and strengthened. A new area of technical intervention—flood protection—is con-templated to decrease vulnerability in areas that may be more prone to sudden fluc-tuations in stream-flow; such fluctuations are becoming more likely under conditions of climate change and exacerbating effects such as vegetation loss from deforestation or drought.

Recommended Priority Protection Actions

Putting into place protective mechanisms often requires a multi-sectoral approach, as seen in the TWRAS. Nonetheless, it is often necessary for single sectors to take a lead role, with support from other ministries. Some national level programs are already in place and could also be enhanced. Within each of the sectors we consider here, it is possible and desirable to provide additional support in all of the areas mentioned: revenue retention schemes; adaptive co-management arrangements; increased education and awareness; implemen-tation of vulnerability monitoring systems; and, various diversification measures for reduc-ing vulnerability to single sector shocks. A sector-by-sector list of potential interventions is provided in the Appendix.

What is more critical at this stage, however, is an overall recognition of the need for disaster management and planning, and development of a comprehensive coordinating function that can promote an overall precautionary approach throughout all sectors. The Tsunami Task Force, for example, is involved in improving emergency response protocols for such disasters. There are resources within the country (such as at the Disaster Man-agement Department of UCLAS) that can assist in training and eventual implementation of various programs. High level coordination is, however, lacking. We thus recommend the establishment of a permanent vulnerability analysis and disaster preparedness unit that is capable of providing coordination and addressing the issues raised in this chapter. Such a unit could report to the President's Office or the Vice President's Office but it is para-mount that it receives adequate resources to provide some coordination and leadership. In addition, this coordinating activity needs to reach down to all districts through the imple-mentation of vulnerability mapping exercises as part of local planning.

CHAPTER 5

Action Plan

Summary of Findings

This review has generally argued that the natural resource sector in Tanzania is dynamic and a potentially important contributor to overall economic growth and poverty alleviation. It does, however, remain fragile and the use of well-placed interventions can serve to secure its role as an engine of growth. In particular, much of sectoral output remains hidden, either because it is not recorded in national statistics, or because potential economic values are either destroyed or squandered as a result of various weaknesses. There is substantial difference among the sectors we have considered here—which include fisheries, forestry, wildlife, tourism, mining and trade in carbon resources—and we have seen that efforts are underway by government in all cases to correct some existing weaknesses.

But the weaknesses persist. We have identified three basic types of weaknesses that are reflected to varying degrees throughout the sector. We characterize these as: poor governance; inefficient management; and, vulnerability:

▓ *Poor governance* is reflected in persistent corruption and lack of transparency in how resources are administered by government. It can arise from the lack of a responsible institution, or from poor record keeping and blatant illegal activities. Governance issues are least serious in freshwater fisheries, tourism, and large-scale mining, and most serious in marine fisheries, forestry, wildlife management, and artisanal mining. Trade in carbon resources suffers from the newness of the activity and the lack of government capacity in the area, but there is no evidence of poor governance through corruption or illegal activity.

■ *Inefficient management* relates to situations where market or policy failures have reduced the value of the resource base or reduced the rent that can be captured effectively by existing mechanisms. The most common inefficiencies arise from unclear property rights, incorrect resource pricing, tax system distortions, and inequitable benefit sharing (which creates conflicts and reduces management effectiveness). Losses associated with inefficient management are currently most significant with marine fisheries and wildlife resources because of resource pricing and property rights issues; similar inefficiencies persist in artisanal mining but these are compounded by social and environmental externalities relating to human health and environmental impacts.

■ *Vulnerability* is a system-wide effect that speaks to the ability of the resource base, and of those dependent on the resource, to withstand unforeseen shocks. These shocks are becoming more frequent, and are related both to internal factors (such as general poverty or dependence on single resources) as well as external factors (such as global security, climate change, and international commodity prices). All sectors are vulnerable, in various ways, to such shocks.

Summary of Recommendations and Priority Actions

Addressing these weaknesses requires an integrated approach, but we highlight three types of interventions that correspond to the different classes of weakness.

The basic foundation (or first pillar) is associated with *reforms that promote good governance*. The elimination of corruption and improved transparency is the foundation for any type of subsequent improvement in resource management. An ideal rent collection system or an optimal fiscal regime is of no use if the overall system is corrupt or lacks basic administrative capacity to monitor and assess activities. While Tanzania has made progress in overall governance, some additional interventions are appropriate. The reforms we focus on the establishment of responsible authorities, on training and human resource development, and on overall transparency and accountability. Another area of potential intervention in this area—judiciary reform—has not been considered in this review.

The second pillar involves *management interventions that improve efficiency* of resource development and exploitation. These presuppose the existence of a regime and administrative structure that reflects good governance. Interventions in this area generally include the creation or enforcement of property rights, correct resource pricing, elimination of distorting taxes and subsidies, and improvement in benefit sharing.

The third pillar we refer to as *protection of the resource base through safety nets*; it is intended to reduce vulnerability of the resource base and the populations that depend on the resource. We treat it separately because the measures are less familiar to planners and, at times, appear to contradict some standard approaches to improving governance or improving efficiency. For example, safety nets and vulnerability reduction often rely on duplication or redundancy to increase system resilience and adaptive capacity. Such duplication may increase costs or administrative burdens, but it is a common feature of safety net mechanisms. The instruments we focus on in the review include revenue retention schemes, adaptive co-management models, education and awareness, vulnerability

Table 5.1. Summary of Objectives, Priority Recommended Actions, and Indicative Results Indicators

Reform: Promoting Good Governance	Management: Improving Efficiency	Protection: Providing Safety Nets
Objective: Eliminate corruption and improve transparency of governance in the sector.	*Objective:* Eliminate market and policy distortions, improve rent capture, and achieve a more equitable distribution of benefits.	*Objective:* Reduce vulnerability of natural resources to shocks, and enhance the resilience of populations dependent on these resources.
Priority Reform Actions for Specific Sectors: ▪ Operationalize Deep Sea Fishing Authority. ▪ Create and Operationalize Executive Agency for Forestry. ▪ Review institutional arrangements affecting Wildlife Division and TANAPA, with a view to establishing a new executive agency in the wildlife sector. ▪ Review capacity and training needs within MEM to improve modalities of artisanal mining governance. ▪ Training and human resource development through use of anti-corruption training programs for lead agencies in all sectors (fisheries, forestry, wildlife, tourism, mining, carbon). ▪ Training in anti-corruption methods at District level and sensitization for implementing partners in NGOs and private sector, particularly in fisheries, forestry, and wildlife. ▪ Enhancements to accounting, monitoring and reporting systems in all sectors. ▪ Accelerated implementation of MCS database for offshore fisheries. ▪ Accelerated establishment of a GPS/GIS mineral cadastral system and database for the mining sector.	*Priority Management Actions for Specific Sectors:* ▪ Strengthen community property rights in wildlife and forestry through implementing more community managed areas. ▪ Establishment of a community territorial sea along coast. ▪ Operationalize cadastral system for artisanal mining. ▪ Establish a legal framework for ownership of carbon resources. ▪ Reform and harmonize licensing system for offshore fisheries, with net increases in fee structures. Consider implementation of bidding system. ▪ Implement an open tendering scheme for wildlife licensing with transparent mechanisms for an appropriate level of domestic preference. ▪ Review of taxation instruments to encourage effective value-added processing in marine fisheries and wildlife products. ▪ Adopt uniform taxation provisions for mining sector in lieu of individually negotiated agreements. ▪ Increase direct involvement of private sector in management of fisheries, wildlife, tourism and mining.	*Priority Coordinating Mechanism:* ▪ Establish a high level coordinating unit to address vulnerability issues at a national level, reporting to the President or Vice President. ▪ Development of vulnerability profiles based on social and natural resource mapping (building on poverty mapping). *Priority Protection Actions:* ▪ Increase use of revenue retention schemes with preference for those involving uncorrelated risks and pooling of revenues (such as the Marine Legacy Fund). ▪ Increase reliance on adaptive co-management arrangements with local communities, private sector, and government. ▪ Development of norms and standards, and support for education and awareness around vulnerable resources. ▪ Implementation of vulnerability monitoring systems, including early warning systems for known threats. ▪ Implement diversification and protection mechanisms for vulnerable groups, focusing on protection of critical ecosystems and guaranteed access to traditional uses of resources.

(Continued)

Table 5.1. Summary of Objectives, Priority Recommended Actions, and Indicative Results Indicators (Continued)

Reform: Promoting Good Governance	Management: Improving Efficiency	Protection: Providing Safety Nets
Key Reform Indicators:	*Key Management Indicators:*	*Key Protection Indicators:*
■ Operational agencies with transparent monitoring and reporting systems in place.	■ Increased proportion of resource subject to managed access (as opposed to open or unmanaged access).	■ An emergency response network and plans in place nationally.
■ Reduced leakages from corruption and illegal activities.	■ Increased rent generation and capture.	■ Poverty and vulnerability mapping being used at District level.
■ Improved awareness regarding good governance among government staff and other stakeholders.	■ Increased participation by local communities in resource management, with increased share of benefits.	■ Monitoring systems in place and delivering timely reports.
	■ Reduced resource use conflicts.	■ Demonstrated positive outcomes in aftermath of unanticipated shocks.

monitoring systems, and diversification. All of these tactics, however, must be coordinated by an overarching strategy of vulnerability management that—at this stage—does not yet exist. A key recommendation of this review is thus to define and institutionalize such a strategy within a central coordinating mechanism in the President's Office or Vice President's Office.

A summary of the recommendations is provided in Table 5.1 which shows the key actions within each of these three pillars. The table is presented as a simplified log-frame or results matrix, including some potential indicative indicators for tracking results and impacts.

Sector-at-a-Glance: Priority Interventions

The following summary tables show priority interventions by sector:

Table A.1. Fisheries (Freshwater)

Intervention	Target	Priority	G: Institutional Reforms	G: Training	G: Transparency and Monitoring Systems	I: Property Right Reforms	I: Resource Pricing Reforms	I: Tax/Subsidy Reforms	I: Supportive institutional Restructuring	V: Revenue Retention	V: Co-management	V: Education/Awareness	V: Vulnerability Monitoring	V: Diversification
Anti-corruption training	trained staff in MNRT (fisheries), relevant districts			*										
Review and enhancements to monitoring systems	timely generation of reports within MNRT (fisheries)				*									
Increased reliance on private sector partnerships to promote sectoral development and value added processing	increased private sector participation, including comanagement ventures with local communities								*		*			
Linkage of fishery levy to other potential revenue retention schemes (e.g., MLF)	secure core financing available for fishery sector									*				
Routine monitoring and reporting on local health and welfare conditions in fishing areas	information inputs to vulnerability database												*	

Education and awareness building regarding use of non-sustainable fishing techniques (such as undersize nets)	decreased illegal fishing						*	*
Establishment of village development plans to identify local diversification opportunities	completed village development plans							*
Other: Linkages to centrally coordinated national vulnerability monitoring and response network	part of national planning and response network managed through VPO/PO.				*	*	*	*

* Objectives include: G: Improve Governance; I: Improve Efficiency; V: Reduce Vulnerability.

Table A.2. Fisheries (Marine)

Intervention	Target	Priority	G: Institutional Reforms	G: Training	G: Transparency and Monitoring Systems	I: Property Right Reforms	I: Resource Pricing Reforms	I: Tax/Subsidy Reforms	I: Supportive institutional Restructuring	V: Revenue Retention	V: Co-management	V: Education/Awareness	V: Vulnerability Monitoring	V: Diversification
Operationalization of the Deep Sea Fishing Authority	an operational DSFA, with links to MNRT, MALE		*		*									
Anti-corruption training	trained staff within MNRT, MALE, related districts, DSFA when operational, partners in private sector and communities			*										
Review and enhancements to MCS systems	effective enforcement capable within MNRT, MALE, DSFA				*									
Establishment of community territorial sea	capacity and regulations in place in districts, management agreements with villages, village development plans reflect sea management					*								

Objective: Input Type*

Item	Benchmark/Target					
Licensing system reform for improved rent capture and compliance monitoring	revenue collection by DSFA increases to $20 million annually	*				
Review of income tax provisions to identify leakages in sector and recommend areas for potential value added processing and revenue retention	completed recommendations		*			
Increased reliance on private sector partnerships to promote sectoral development and value added processing	increased private sector participation, including comanagement ventures with local communities			*		
establishment of Marine Legacy Fund, including revenues from non-fisheries activities	preliminary fund and modalities in place in 2007, with target of US$1 million in fund by 2009				*	
Increased reliance on comanagement arrangements for establishment of locally managed areas					*	*
Routine monitoring and reporting on local health and welfare conditions in fishing areas	information inputs to vulnerability database					*
Other: Linkages to centrally coordinated national vulnerability monitoring and response network	part of national planning and response network managed through VPO/PO.			*	*	*

* Objectives include: G: Improve Governance; I: Improve Efficiency; V: Reduce Vulnerability.

Table A.3. Forestry

Intervention	Target	Priority	G: Institutional Reforms	G: Training	G: Transparency and Monitoring Systems	I: Property Right Reforms	I: Resource Pricing Reforms	I: Tax/Subsidy Reforms	I: Supportive institutional Restructuring	V: Revenue Retention	V: Co-management	V: Education/Awareness	V: Vulnerability Monitoring	V: Diversification
								Objective: Input Type*					
Creation of an Executive Agency responsible for Forestry	An operational new EA, with links to MNRT, TANAPA, districts		*		*									
Anti-corruption training	trained staff in MNRT and related districts, and in the new EA when operational. Effective engagement of these organizations with partners in private sector and communities			*										
Review and enhancements to monitoring systems	Effective monitoring and enforcement capable within MNRT				*									
Establishment of national inventory	Regular reporting from inventory				*									

Activity	Rationale						
Establishment of a revenue retention framework within the new EA that is linked to other revenue retention schemes, and involves distributions to local districts	secure core funding for the sector			*			
Routine monitoring and reporting on local health and welfare conditions in forest areas	information inputs to vulnerability database					*	
Other: Linkages to centrally coordinated national vulnerability monitoring and response network	part of national planning and response network managed through VPO/PO.		*	*	*	*	*

* Objectives include: G: Improve Governance; I: Improve Efficiency; V: Reduce Vulnerability.

Table A.4. Wildlife

Intervention	Target	Priority	Objective: Input Type*											
			G: Institutional Reforms	G: Training	G: Transparency and Monitoring Systems	I: Property Right Reforms	I: Resource Pricing Reforms	I: Tax/Subsidy Reforms	I: Supportive institutional Restructuring	V: Revenue Retention	V: Co-management	V: Education/Awareness	V: Vulnerability Monitoring	V: Diversification
Institutional review of Wildlife Department and Tanapa, with a view to establishing an executive agency.	Completed recommendations regarding potential restructuring options for MNRT, TANAPA, and districts		*		*									
Anti-corruption training	Staff trained in MNRT, TANAPA, related districts, and the new EA if applicable. Interactions with relevant partners in private sector and communities.			*										
Review and enhancements to monitoring systems	Effective reporting in MNRT under domestic and international obligations, with information base capable of use for prosecutions				*									
Changes in wildlife licensing to permit open market auctions, with appropriate and transparent domestic-preference provisions	Secure licenses held by a diversity of foreign and domestic firms with clear joint venture partnerships, taxable by TRA						*							

Activity	Target/Output						
Review of income tax provisions to identify leakages in sector and recommend areas for potential value added processing and revenue retention	completed recommendations	*					
Increased reliance on private sector partnerships to promote sectoral development and value added processing	increased private sector participation, including comanagement ventures with local communities		*				
Establishment of a transparent revenue retention framework within the sector that is linked to other revenue retention schemes, and involves distributions to local districts	secure core funding for the sector			*			
Review of establishing a revenue retention scheme for E African parks (with Uganada Wildlife Authority and Kenya Wildlife Service)	completed review; secure funding of TANAPA			*			
Implementation of Wildlife Managament Areas	increased number of WMAs with local participation			*	*	*	*
Routine monitoring and reporting on local health and welfare conditions in wildlife areas	information inputs to vulnerability database					*	
Other: Linkages to centrally coordinated national vulnerability monitoring and response network	part of national planning and response network managed through VPO/PO.			*	*	*	*

* Objectives include: G: Improve Governance; I: mprove Efficiency; V: Reduce Vulnerability.

Table A.5. Tourism

Intervention	Target	Priority	G: Institutional Reforms	G: Training	G: Transparency and Monitoring Systems	I: Property Right Reforms	I: Resource Pricing Reforms	I: Tax/Subsidy Reforms	I: Supportive Institutional Restructuring	V: Revenue Retention	V: Co-management	V: Education/Awareness	V: Vulnerability Monitoring	V: Diversification
Anti-corruption training	Trained staff in MNRT			*										
Review and enhancements to monitoring systems	Operational reporting system with timely reports in MNRT				*									
Increased reliance on private sector partnerships to promote sectoral development	increased private sector participation, including comanagement ventures with local communities								*					
Incorporation of a tourism strategy into rural development strategy, reflected in village development plans	icreased diversification and participation of local communities in tourism sector									*	*	*		*
Routine monitoring and reporting on local health and welfare conditions in tourism areas	information inputs to vulnerability database												*	
Other: Linkages to centrally coordinated national vulnerability monitoring and response network	part of national planning and response network managed through VPO/PO.									*	*	*	*	*

* Objectives include: G: Improve Governance; I: Improve Efficiency; V: Reduce Vulnerability.

Table A.6. Mining (Large Scale)

Intervention	Target	Priority	G: Institutional Reforms	G: Training	G: Transparency and Monitoring Systems	I: Property Right Reforms	I: Resource Pricing Reforms	I: Tax/Subsidy Reforms	I: Supportive institutional Restructuring	V: Revenue Retention	V: Co-management	V: Education/Awareness	V: Vulnerability Monitoring	V: Diversification
Review and enhancements to monitoring systems	Timely reporting within MEM				*									
Reform of income tax provisions to ensure uniform application of these provisions to all new mining investments	completed recommendations							*						
Review of revenue retention schemes in mineral and mining sector, with a view to improving distribution at local level that minimizes disruptions from mining	completed recommendations									*				
Initiate within village development plans contingency measures for impacts and mine closures	comprehensive village development plans										*			*
Initiate education and awareness programs regarding negative impacts of child labor; complement with enforcement and standards	reduced child labor								*			*		

(Continued)

71

Table A.6. Mining (Large Scale) (Continued)

Intervention	Target	Priority	G: Institutional Reforms	G: Training	G: Transparency and Monitoring Systems	I: Property Right Reforms	I: Resource Pricing Reforms	I: Tax/Subsidy Reforms	I: Supportive institutional Restructuring	V: Revenue Retention	V: Co-management	V: Education/Awareness	V: Vulnerability Monitoring	V: Diversification
Imposition of basic hygienic standards such as proper drinking water; safety standards; malaria action program	improved health standards											*		
Commence routine monitoring of local health conditions in large-scale mining areas	information flowing into national vulnerability information systems												*	
Other: Linkages to centrally coordinated national vulnerability monitoring and response network	part of national planning and response network managed through VPO/PO.									*	*	*	*	*

* Objectives include: G: Improve Governance; I: Improve Efficiency; V: Reduce Vulnerability.

Table A.7. Mining (Artisanal)

Intervention	Target	Priority	G: Institutional Reforms	G: Training	G: Transparency and Monitoring Systems	I: Property Right Reforms	I: Resource Pricing Reforms	I: Tax/Subsidy Reforms	I: Supportive institutional Restructuring	V: Revenue Retention	V: Co-management	V: Education/Awareness	V: Vulnerability Monitoring	V: Diversification
						Objective: Input Type*								
MEM capacity review to identify training needs.	Training plan for MEM and districts to improve awarenss and governance of small-scale mining activities.			*	*									
Anti-corruption training	Trained staff within MEM, and mining districts			*										
Establishment of GPS/GIS mineral cadastral system	Within MEM, an operational cadastral system capable of tracking licenses and general use of land.				*	*								
Increased reliance on private sector partnerships to promote sectoral development and value added processing	increased private sector participation, including comanagement ventures with local communities								*					
Review of revenue retention schemes in mineral and mining sector, with a view to improving distribution at local level that minimizes disruptions from mining	completed recommendations										*			

(Continued)

Table A.7. Mining (Artisanal) (Continued)

Intervention	Target	Priority	G: Institutional Reforms	G: Training	G: Transparency and Monitoring Systems	I: Property Right Reforms	I: Resource Pricing Reforms	I: Tax/Subsidy Reforms	I: Supportive institutional Restructuring	V: Revenue Retention	V: Co-management	V: Education/Awareness	V: Vulnerability Monitoring	V: Diversification
Initiate village development plans in areas prone to artisanal mining, including contingency measures for mining impacts	comprehensive village development plans										*			*
Initiate education and awareness programs regarding negative impacts of child labor; complement with enforcement and standards	reduced child labor								*			*		
Imposition of basic hygienic standards in mining areas such as proper drinking water; safety standards; malaria action program	improved health standards											*		
Commence routine monitoring of local health conditions in artisanal mining areas	information flowing into national vulnerability information systems												*	

Activity	Objective								
Provide information and training for health care providers regarding mercury health effects to pregnant women, children, mercury intoxication and medical treatment, etc	improved local health conditions						*		
Implement a "mercury ambulance" for small-scale miners instead of permanent local health office	reduced mortality/morbidity from mercury poisoning				*		*		
Other: Linkages to centrally coordinated national vulnerability monitoring and response network	part of national planning and response network managed through VPO/PO.			*	*		*	*	*

* Objectives include: G: Improve Governance; I: Improve Efficiency; V: Reduce Vulnerability.

Table A.8. Carbon Resources

Intervention	Target	Priority	G: Institutional Reforms	G: Training	G: Transparency and Monitoring Systems	I: Property Right Reforms	I: Resource Pricing Reforms	I: Tax/Subsidy Reforms	I: Supportive institutional Restructuring	V: Revenue Retention	V: Co-management	V: Education/Awareness	V: Vulnerability Monitoring	V: Diversification
Creation and strengthening of a national focal office for carbon resources	Operational staffed office reporting to VPO		*	*										
Institutional support to line agencies, municipalities and districts regarding carbon resource trading	Trained staff within following agencies: NEMC, MNRT (Forestry), MEM (Energy), selected districts and municipalities			*										
Review and reform of policy, legislation and regulations regarding carbon resource property rights; community rights defined in this framework	Clear property rights over carbon resources reflected in MOUs or similar operational co-management agreements					*					*			
Anti-corruption training	Trained staff within a new national focal office, and in NEMC			*										
Creation of a monitoring database consistent with international verification requirements	Establishment of database within new national focal office				*									
Other: Linkages to centrally coordinated national vulnerability monitoring and response network	part of national planning and response network managed through VPO/PO.									*	*	*	*	*

* Objectives include: G: Improve Governance; I: Improve Efficiency; V: Reduce Vulnerability.

References

Anglogold, Ashanti. 2005. Case studies—Tanzania: Understanding and working with artisanal miners in Africa. 05 Report to Society. http://www.anglogold.co.za/subwebs/ InformationForInvestors/ReportToSociety05/values_bus_principles/community/c_cs_ tzn_5_5.htm

Appleton, J.D., H. Taylor, T.R. Lister, and B. Smith. 2004. "Assessment of the Environment in the Rwamagasa area, Tanzania, Final Report, Tanzania." UNIDO Project EG/GLO/01/ G34, British Geological Survey/National Environment Research Council, Nottingham.

COWI. 2005. *Study on Growth and Environment Links for Preparation of Country Economic Memorandum—Final Report.* 3 Volumes. Dar es Salaam.

Diamond Development Initiative (DDI). 2005. Mission Statement. http://www.diamonds .net/news/NewsItem.aspx?ArticleID=12992

FAO. 2006. *Review of the State of the World Fisheries Management: Indian Ocean.* FAO Fisheries Technical Paper 488. Rome.

Foreign Investment Advisory Service (FIAS). 2006. "Sector Study of the Effective Tax Burden: Tanzania."

International Institute for Environment and Development (IIED) and the World Business Council for Sustainable Development (WBCSD). 2002. *Small-scale Mining and Sustainable Development within the SADC Region.*

International Monetary Fund. 2004. *Tanzania: Selected Issues and Statistical Appendix.* Country Report 04/284. http://www.imf.org/external/pubs/ft/scr/2004/cr04284 .pdf#search=%22IMF%20country%20report%2004%2F284%22.

MNRT (Ministry of Natural Resources and Tourism). 2006. Government comments on COWI report—Harvesting natural resources for sustainable and shared growth in Tanzania. Ref AB176/315/0—T.F. Kilenga Ag. Permanent Secretary, July 24th.

Noack, F., and J. Ruitenbeek. Forthcoming 2007. "Coupling and decoupling strategies for natural resource management in East Africa."

Phillips, L., H. Semboja, G.P. Shukla, R. Sezinga, W. Mutagwaba, B. Mchwampaka, G. Wanga, G. Kahyarara, and P.C. Keller. 2001. "Tanzania's Precious Minerals Boom: Issues in Mining and Marketing." Research Paper, USAID Bureau for Africa. Office of Sustainable Development. Washington.

Plummer, R., and D. Armitage. 2006. "Charting the new territory of Adaptive Co-management: Synthesis of the Delphi Results."

Schneider, Friedrich. 2002. "Size and measurement of the informal economy in 110 countries."

Walley, Christine J. 2004. *Rough waters: Nature and development in an East African marine park.* Princeton: Princeton University Press.

World Bank, UNCTAD Commodities Branch, and the International Council on Mining and Minerals (ICMM). 2006. "The Challenge of Mineral Wealth: using resource endowments to foster sustainable development. Synthesis of four Country Case Studies."

World Bank. 2006a. "Tanzania—Water Resources Assistance Strategy."

———. 2006b. *Where is the Wealth of Nations: Measuring Capital for the 21st Century.* Washington, D.C.

Consolidated sources from COWI (2005) Report

Abila, R.O. 2000. *The Development of the Lake Victoria Fishery. A Boon or Bane for Food Security?* IUCN, The World Conservation Union.

Abila, R.O., and E.G. Jansen. 1997. *From Local to Global Market. The Fish Exporting and Fishmeal Industries of Lake Victoria Structure, Strategies and Socio-economic Impacts in Kenya.* IUCN, The World Conservation Union.

Ashley, C., N. Mdoe, and L. Reynolds. 2002. "Rethinking Wildlife for Livelihoods and Diversification in Rural Tanzania: A Case Study from Northern Selous." LADDER Working Paper 15, University of East Anglia, Norwich.

Atkinson, G., and K. Hamilton. 2003. "Savings, growth and the resource curse hypothesis." *World Development* 31(11):1793–1807.

Auty, R.M. 1997. "Sustaining development in mineral economies: the resource curse thesis." *Journal of International Development* 9(4):651–63.

Barnett, R., ed. 2000. *Food for Thought: The Utilization of Wild Meat in Eastern and Southern Africa.* Nairobi: TRAFFIC East/Southern Africa.

Barrick Gold Corporation. 2005. "Heart of Gold Fund."

Bokea, C. Ikiara. 2000. *The Macro economy of the Export Fishing Industry in Lake Victoria (Kenya).* IUCN, The World Conservation Union.

Boschini, A., J. Pettersson, and J. Roine. 2003. "Resource curse or not: A question of appropriability." Working Paper in Economics and Finance 534, Stockholm School of Economics, Stockholm.

Bravo-Ortega, C., and J. De Gregorio. Undated. "The Relative Richness of the Poor? Natural Resources, Human Capital and Economic Growth." Working Paper Central Bank of Chile 139, Central Bank of Chile, Santiago de Chile.

Buys, H., I. Moshi, and Mariki. 1996. "Long-term Financing of Forestry." Report prepared for FCMP.

Cavendish, W. 1999. "Empirical Regularities in the Poverty-Environment Relationship of African Rural Household." Working Paper 99-21, University of Oxford, Oxford.

CEEST (Centre for Energy, Environment, Science and Technology). Undated. "Environmental impacts of small scale Mining: A case study of Merelani, Kahama, Nzega, Geita and Musoma." CEEST Research Report 1, Dar es Salaam.

Cervellati, M., and P. Fortunato. 2004. "Natural resources and the wealth of nations in a globalized world economy." Cahiers de la MSE 04068, Maison des Sciences Economiques, Université Paris Panthéon-Sorbonne, Paris.

Chatterjee, Mushi. 1994. "Study on improvement and monitoring royalty collection systems." Report 1, Evaluation, reformulation and design of recommendations of the Silviconsult study.

Chopin, F. 2005. "Review and assessment of the DRAFT United Republic of Tanzania–European Community Fisheries Agreement." Draft.

Dasgupta, S., with U. Deichmann, C. Meisner, and D. Wheeler. 2003. "The Poverty/Environment Nexus in Cambodia and Lao People's Democratic Republic." Policy Research Working Paper Series 2960, The World Bank, Washington, D.C.

De Long, J.B., and J.G. Williamson. 1994. "Natural Resources and Convergence in the 19th and 20th Centuries." Harvard University. Processed.

DFID. 2002. "Better livelihoods for poor people: The role of agriculture, Issues Paper—Consultation Document." Prepared by DFID Rural Livelihoods Department, Department for International Development, London.

———. 2003. "Just Wildlife? Or a Source of local Development?" ODI Natural Resource Perspectives 85.

DPG. 2005. "Brief on Issues Pertaining to Tourist Hunting." Development Partners Group Tanzania.

Drasch, G., and S. Boese-O'Reilly. 2004. "Assessment of health in the Rwamagasa area, Tanzania, in Final Report for an Assessment of the Environment and Health in the Rwamagasa area, Tanzania." UNIDO Project EG/GLO/01/G34, Nottingham: British Geological Survey/National Environment Research Council.

EIU (Economist Intelligence Unit). 2004. *Tanzania—Country Profile 2004*. London.

Emmanuel, J. 2001. "Tourism in Mikumi National Park (MNRP) Morogoro, Tanzania."

Eustack, M.B. 2004. "Assessment of the contribution of agroforestry to poverty alleviation in Lushoto District." MSc Thesis.

George, A.K.N. 2003. "Socio-Economic Impacts of Mining on the Livelihood of Local Communities in Geita District, Tanzania." MA Dissertation, Sokoine University of Agriculture.

Gibbon, P. 1997. "Of saviours and punks: The political economy of the Nile Perch marketing chain in Tanzania." CDR Working Paper 97.3, June.

Gillingham, S. 1998. "Giving Wildlife Value: A Case Study of Community Wildlife Management Around Selous Game Reserve, Tanzania." Dissertation submitted to the University College of Cambridge.

Government of Tanzania. 2005. "National Strategy for Growth and Reduction of Poverty."

Grossman, G.M., and A.B. Krueger. 1991. *The Environmental Impact of the North American Free Trade Agreement*. Working Paper 3914. Cambridge, Mass.: National Bureau of Economic Research.

———. 1995. "Economic Growth and the Environment." *Quarterly Journal of Economics* 110:353–77.

Gylfason T. 2000. *Resources, Agriculture, and Economic Growth in Economies in Transition*. CERGE-EI Working Paper 157. Prague: The Center for Economic Research and Graduate Education—Economic Institute.

Gylfason, T., T.T. Herbertsson, and G. Zoega. 1997. *A Mixed Blessing: Natural Resources and Economic Growth*. C.E.P.R. Discussion Paper 1668. London: Centre for Economic Policy Research.

Gylfason, T., and G. Zoega. 2001. *Natural Resources and Economic Growth: The Role of Investment*. C.E.P.R. Discussion Paper 2743. London: Centre for Economic Policy Research.

Hangi, A.Y. 2001. "Tanzania's pot of gold" news.bbc.co.uk, July 22nd.

Heltberg, R., and U. Nielsen. 2000. "Foreign aid, development and the environment." In Finn Tarp, ed., *Foreign Aid and Development*. London: Routledge.

Hoadley, M., D. Limpitlaw, and A. Weaver. 2002. *Mining, Minerals and Sustainable Development in southern Africa—Volume 1: The Report of the Regional MMSD Process.* Wits: University of the Witwatersrand.

Hodler, R. 2004. *The Curse of Natural Resources in Fractionalized Countries.* Diskussionsschriften 0404. Bern: Universität Bern.

Homewood, K., E.F. Lambin, E. Coast, and Kariuki. 2001. "Long Term Changes in Serengeti-Mara Wildebeest and Land Cover: Pastoralism, Population or Policies?" *PNAS* 98(22).

Idda, M.A. 2003. "Contribution of Agroforestry to human nutrition. A case of Arusha Region." MSc Thesis.

IMF. 2004. *Tanzania—Selected Issues and Statistical Appendix.* Washington.

Issango, J. 2001. "Honey production and sales along Dar es Salaam—Morogoro Highway."

IUCN. 2000. "The effectiveness of trade measures contained in the convention on international trade in endangered species of wild fauna and flora." UNEP Economics, Trade and Environment Unit.

Jambiya, G., K. Kulindwa, and H. Sosovele. 1997. *Poverty and the Environment: Informal Sand-mining, Quarrying and Lime-making.* Policy Brief 97.1. Dar es Salaam: Research on Poverty Alleviation.

Jansen, E.G. 1997. "Rich fisheries poor fisherfolk: Some preliminary observation about the effects of trade and aid in the Lake Victoria fisheries." IUCN, The World Conservation Union.

Jansen, E.G., R.O. Abila, and J.P. Owino. 1999. "Constraints and opportunities for 'Community Participation' in the management of the Lake Victoria fisheries." IUCN, The World Conservation Union.

Kaduvage, B.L. 2000. "Study on the present status and future prospects for mechanical and chemical industries in Tanzania, Project report."

Kagya, M.A. 2002. "Contribution of non-wood forest products to household economy and welfare of women in Meatu District, Shinyanga Region, Tanzania." MSc Thesis.

———. 2004. "Gums and Resins production and marketing in Tanzania. FAO project report, Strengthening the Production and Quality Control of Gums and Resins in Africa."

Kallonga, E., A. Rodgers, F. Nelson, Y. Ndoinyo, and N. Rugemeleza. 2003. "Reforming Environmental Governance in Tanzania: Natural Resource Management and the Rural Economy." Non-commissioned paper presented at the Inaugural Tanzania Biennial Development Forum, April 24–25th, Dar es Salaam.

Khamis, F.A. 2003. "Financial Analysis of Ecotourism industry. A case study of Jozani-Chwaka Bay conservation area, Zanzibar."

Kobb, D. 1999. "Forestry royalties in Tanga Region: Paper vs. Reality." Paper prepared for East Usambara Catchment Forestry Project, Natural Resources Management and Buffer Zone Development Program, Tanga Coastal Zone.

Koppers, B. 1998. "End of Assignment Report, Danagro."

Korongo, Ltd. 2003. "Poverty and the Environment in Tanzania—A Preliminary Study of Environment and Poverty Linkages. Study commissioned by the World Bank, Dar es Salaam Country Office.

Kowero. 1990. "Some Aspects of Tanzanian Forest Royalties." TFAP, Working Paper 26, Forestry and Beekeeping Division.

———. 1991. "Management and utilisation of forest estate in Tanzania: Some policy issues." *Journal of World Forest Resource Management* 8(10):15–27.

KRCD. 2005. "Establishment of a socio-economic monitoring system for WMAs. Mission report." Unpublished.

Kudoja. W. 2004. "LVFRP conducting sonar fish surveys in Lake Victoria." *ICT update: A current awareness bulletin for ACP agriculture* Issue 16(March).

Kulindwa, K. 2001. "The Contribution of Lake Victoria Fisheries to the National Economy." A report submitted to LVEMP, Fisheries Research Component, Socio-economic sub-component.

Kulindwa, K., O. Mashindano, F. Shechambo, and H. Sosovele. 2003. "Mining for Sustainable Development in Tanzania." Economic Research Bureau, Dar es Salaam.

Kulindwa, K., H. Sosovele, and O. Mashindano. 2001. *Tourism Growth for Sustainable Development in Tanzania.* Dar es Salaam University Press.

Kweka, J., O. Morrissey, and A. Blake. 2003. "The economic potential of tourism in Tanzania." *Journal of International Development.*

Lane, P., and A. Tornell. 1995. "Power Concentration and Growth." Discussion Paper 1720, Harvard Institute of Economic Research.

Lange, G.-M., H.R. Hassan, and K. Hamilton. 2003. *Environmental Accounting in Action case studies from Southern Africa.* Cheltenham: Edward Edgar.

Law Reform Commission. 2001. "Position paper on the legal framework for the development of the mining industry."

Luoga, E.J., E.T.F. Witkowski, and K. Balkwill. 2000. "Economics of charcoal production in Miombo woodland of eastern Tanzania: Some hidden costs associated with commercialization of the resources." *Ecol Econ* 35:243–57.

Lusambo, L.P. 2002. "Socio-Economic Analysis of Land use Factors causing Degradation and Deforestation of Miombo Woodlands. Case Study of Kilosa District, Tanzania." MSc Thesis.

Lyimo, J.O. 2002. "Production economics of Transmission poles in Tanzania."

Mabugu, R., and P. Mugoya. 2001. "Financing, Revenue sharing and Taxation issues in Wildlife Management Areas." Report prepared for USAID.

MacAlister, Elliot, and Partners. 1999. "Regional Socio-economic Studies on Employment and the Level of Dependency on Fishing. Greece (Lot II). Final Report, Nov." European Commission DGXIV (Fisheries).

Makundi, W.R., and A. O'kting'ati. 1991. "Carbon flows and economic evaluation of mitigation options in Tanzania's forest sector."

Malimbwi, R.E., S. Misana, G.C. Monela, G. Jambiya, and E. Zahabu. 2000. "Socio-economics of charcoal extraction to the forest resources of Tanzania: The case study of Kitulangalo Area, Tanzania."

Martinussen, J.D. 1999. Samfund, Stat og Marked, Mllemfolkeligt Samvirke. Copenhagen.

Matsuyama, K. 1992. "Agricultural productivity, comparative advantage, and economic growth." *Journal of Economic Theory* 58:317–34.

Mkanta, Chimtembo. 2002. "Towards Natural Resource Accounting in Tanzania, A study on the Contribution of Natural Forests to National Income." CEEPA Discussion Paper Series.

MNRT (Ministry of Natural Resources and Tourism). 2000. "Lake Victoria Frame Survey Results."

———. 2001a. "National Forest Programme in Tanzania (2001–2010)." Forestry and Beekeeping Division.

————. 2001b. "National Beekeeping Programme (2001–2010)." Forestry and Beekeeping Division.

————. 2002. "Forestry in Figures." Forestry and Beekeeping Division.

————. 2004. "MTEF Budget of the Ministry of Natural Resources and Tourism, Vote 69."

Monela, G.C., S.A.O. Chamshama, R. Mwaipopo, and D.M. Gamassa. 2004. "A study on the social, economic, and environmental impacts of forest landscape restoration in Shinyanga Region." MNRT & IUCN.

Mugurusi, E.K. 2002. "Tourism Investment Forum." Dar es Salaam.

Mushi, J.A. 1999. "Evaluation of Revnue Collection and Monitoring Systems in Singida, Tabora, Shinyanga, and Mwanza Regions." Report prepared for Forest Resources Management Project (FRMP), IDA Credit no. 2335-TA.

Mutagwaba, W., R. Mwipopo-Ako, and A. Mlaki. 1997. *Poverty and Technology: The Case of Artisanal Mining*. Policy Brief No. 97-2. Dar es Salaam: Research on Poverty Alleviation.

Mwaipopo, R., W. Mutagwaba, and D. Nyange, with E. Fisher. 2004. "Increasing the Contribution of Artisanal and Small-scale Mining to Poverty Reduction in Tanzania—Based on an Analysis of Mining Livelihoods in Misungwi and Geita Districts, Mwanza region." Prepared for DFID.

Mwalyosi, R.B.B. 2004. "Impact Assessment and the Mining Industry: Perspectives from Tanzania." Presentation made at 2004 IAIA, Vancouver, Canada.

Mwanahija, S.S. 2003. "Contribution of agroforestry vs rural households food insecurity in Kibaha District, Coast Region, Tanzania." MSc Thesis.

National Bureau of Statistics. 2001. *Integrated Labour Force Survey, 2000/01—Analytical Report*. Dar es Salaam.

Ngaga, Y.M. 1990. "Present consumption and future requirement of sawn wood in two urban centers of Tanzania." MSc Thesis.

————. 1998. "Analysis of Production and trade in Forest products of Tanzania." Doctoral Scientiarium Thesis. Department of Forest Sciences, Agricultural University of Norway.

Ngaga, Y.M., S.A.O. Chamshama, and G.C. Monela. 2003. *Resource Economic Analysis of Catchment Forest Reserves in Tanzania.*

Noah, E. 2002. "Impact of production and consumption of wood fuel in Miombo woodlands of Makanya Division, in Kilimanjaro Region."

Noel, M. 2001. "Statistics of game hunting and revenues; and its implication to the economy of Tanzania 1997–2000."

Norconsult. 2002. "The True Cost of Charcoal."

O'kting'ati, A., G.C. Monela, and H. Nyella. 2000. "Contribution of Kilimanjaro Regional Forest Sector to the Economy of Tanzania (1990–1998)."

Papyrakis, E., and G. Reyer. 2004a. "Natural Resources, Innovation, and Growth." Working Paper 2004.129, Fondazione Eni Enrico Mattei, Milan.

————. 2004b. "Natural Resources, Investment and Long-Term Income." Working Paper 2004.87, Fondazione Eni Enrico Mattei, Milan.

Paullo, T. 2002. "Market survey and economic values of useful edible mushrooms consumed in Iringa Municipal."

Pearce, David. 2004. "Growth and environment: can we have both?" *Environment Matters 2004 Annual Review*: 14–15.

Philbert, M. 2002. "Impact of tourism on employment. A case study of Kilimanjaro National Park (KINAPA)."

Phillips, L., H. Semboja, G.P. Shukla, R. Sezinga, W. Mutagwaba, and B. Mchwampaka, with G. Wanga, and G. Kahyarara. 2001a. *Tanzania's Precious Minerals Boom—Issues in Mining and Marketing*. Dar es Salaam: Economic and Social Research Foundation and Arlington: International Business Initiatives Corp.

Phillips, L., R. Sezinga, H. Semboja, and G. Kahyarara. 2001b. "Growth and Equity: Gemstone and Gold Mining in Tanzania." EAGER Policy Brief 56.

Robert, M. 2003. "Economic potential of trophy export in Tanzania."

Roe, D., T. Mulliken, S. Milledge, J. Mremi, S. Mosha, and M. Grieg-Gran. 2002. "Making a killing or making a living? Wildlife trade, trade controls and rural livelihoods." *Biodiversity and Livelihoods* Issues 6, Traffic, IIED.

Ruitenbeek, J., I. Hewawasam, and M. Ngoile, eds. 2005. "Blueprint 2050: Sustaining the Marine Environment in Mainland Tanzania and Zanzibar." The World Bank, Washington, D.C.

Rutenge, C. 2004. "Assessment of the influences of live small animals trade in Arusha Region."

Sachs, J.D., and A.M. Warner. 1995. *Natural Resources Abundance and Economic Growth*. NBER Working Paper 5398. Cambridge, Mass.: National Bureau of Economic Research.

———. 2001. "The curse of natural resources." *European Economic Review* 46:827–38.

Salmi and Monela. 2000. "Study on Financing in Forestry, Formulation of National Forest Programme in Tanzania." Final Report for Ministry of Natural Resources and Tourism (MNRT), Forestry and Beekeeping Division.

Sathaye, J., and W.R. Makundi. 1995. "Biomass and Bio-energy." Special issue forestry and climate change.

Sekandende, A.N. 2001. "Economic benefits of wildlife-based tourism. A case study of Tarangire National Park."

Severin, A. 2001. "The economic implication of tourism towards the economy of Tanzania."

Silviconsult. 1991. "Forest revenue collection in Tanzania." FBD, The World Bank, and ODA.

Skage, Naess. 1994. "Pitsawing and sustainable forest management, a case study of ecological and social considerations from Morogoro District." MSc Thesis in Forestry, Dept. of Forestry, AUN.

Smith, I. Undated. "Welfare, Growth and Environment: A Sceptical Review of the Skeptical Environmentalist." Discussion Paper 0204, University of St. Andrews.

Stijns, J.-P. 2001. *Natural Resource Abundance and Economic Growth Revisited*. University of California at Berkeley.

TANAPA (Tanzania National Parks). 1999. "Review of Efficiency and Effectiveness." Draft Report.

———. Undated. "Maximizing Revenues in Tanzania National Parks: Towards a better understanding of park choice and nature tourism in Tanzania."

Tassell, A. 2004. *Tanzania's gold boom continues*. Johannesburg: Brooke Patrick Publications.

TaTEDO. 2003. "Scaling-up Dissemination, Partnership and Networking for Increased uptake and use of Sustainable Energy Technologies. Annual Report 2002/2003."

Theostina, A.L. 2003. "The role of NTFPs in household food security and women income in Morogoro rural."

Turpie, J.K. 2000. "The use and value of natural resources of the Rufiji floodplain and delta, Rufiji district, Tanzania." Rufiji Environmental Management Project, Dar es Salaam, Technical Report 17.

UNIDO. 2002. "FEATURE: Artisanal Gold Mining without Mercury Pollution." Vienna.

URT (United Republic of Tanzania). 1997a. "Mineral Policy of Tanzania."

———. 1997b. "Ruvuma Region Socio-economic Profile." Dar es Salaam.

———. 1998. "Mining Act."

———. 2002a. "The 2002/2003 Tanzania Participatory Poverty Assessment." http://www
.esrftz.org/ppa.

———. 2002b. "The Masterplan Study on Fisheries Development in the United Republic
of Tanzania. Main Report." Dar es Salaam: JICA/MNRT.

———. 2002c. "Poverty and Human Development Report 2002."

———. 2004a. Budgetary Speech (2004/2005) by the Minister for Natural Resources and
Tourism.

———. 2004b. "Economic Survey for 2003." Dar es Salaam: Planning and Privatisation
Commission.

———. 2004c. "Public Expenditure Review of Environment, Financial Year 2004."

———. 2005. "National Strategy for Growth and Poverty Reduction (NSGRP), United
Republic of Tanzania." Final draft January 15th. Vice President's Office.

———. Undated. "Mining." http://www.tanzania.go.tz/mining.html.

Utz, R. 2005. "Tanzania, recent growth performance and prospects."

Van Campenhout, B. 2002. "The mining industry and the future development of Tanzania."
Prepared for workshop on Globalisation and East Africa, April 15–16, Economic and
Social Research Foundation, Dar es Salaam.

Van Straaten, P. 2000. "Mercury contamination associated with small-scale gold mining
in Tanzania and Zimbabwe." Department of Land Resource Science, University of
Guelph, Guelph.

Verbeke, T., and M. De Clercq. 2003. "The income-environment relationship: Does a logit
model offer an alternative empirical strategy?" Faculty of Economics and Business
Administration, Working Paper 03/192, Ghent University, Ghent.

Vosti, S.A., and T. Reardon. 2001. "Sustainability, growth and poverty alleviation: A policy
and agroecological perspective." Food Policy Statements 25, International Food Policy
Research Institute, Washington, D.C.

Walsh, M.T. 2000. "The development of community wildlife management in Tanzania:
Lessons learned from the Ruaha Ecosystem." Paper presented to the conference on
African Wildlife Management in the New Millennium College of African Wildlife
Management, Mweka, Tanzania, December 13–15.

Williamson, R. 2003. "Private foreign investment and the poorest countries." Paper based
on the Wilton Park Conference Wilton Park Paper 707 on Private Foreign Investment
and the Poorest Countries, Wilton House, West Sussex.

World Bank. 2001. "Tanzania: Women in the mining sector, findings." Washington, D.C.

———. 2002. *World Development Report 2003: Sustainable Development in a Dynamic
World.* Washington, D.C.

———. 2005. "Concept Note for the Tanzania CEM/Poverty Assessment." September
13th.

Yager, T.R. 2003. "The mineral industry of Tanzania." In *U.S. Geological Survey Minerals
Yearbook 2003.*

Eco-Audit

Environmental Benefits Statement

The World Bank is committed to preserving Endangered Forests and natural resources. We print World Bank Working Papers and Country Studies on 100 percent postconsumer recycled paper, processed chlorine free. The World Bank has formally agreed to follow the recommended standards for paper usage set by Green Press Initiative—a nonprofit program supporting publishers in using fiber that is not sourced from Endangered Forests. For more information, visit www.greenpressinitiative.org.

In 2007, the printing of these books on recycled paper saved the following:

Trees*	Solid Waste	Water	Net Greenhouse Gases	Total Energy
264	12,419	96,126	23,289	184 mil.
'40' in height and 6–8" in diameter	Pounds	Gallons	Pounds CO$_2$ Equivalent	BTUs

green press
INITIATIVE